"What keeps us trapped by the mistakes of the pas̲ ̲.̲.̲.̲ ̲.̲.̲.̲.̲ ̲.̲t̲ ̲i̲s̲ ̲t̲h̲e̲ inability to imagine the world being truly different, a lack of example or inspiration to follow, or simply not believing that we can make a difference. The Future Is Beautiful from Think Act Vote has a cure for each of these ills."

Andrew Simms, New Economics Foundation

THINK ACT VOTE

"Martin Luther King did not stand on the steps of the Lincoln Memorial and say "I have a plan". Without dreams of a better future we are destined to the obedience of cynicism, and a miserable life that is. Eleanor Roosevelt nailed it: "The future belongs to those who believe in the beauty of their dreams" - people like the contributors to, and the readers of, this inspiring book"."

Mark Stevenson, author

"Every revolution needs and creates a book. A beautiful revolution needs and creates a beautiful book. This book is it. Buy it, steal it, borrow it, share it and be beautiful."

Neal Lawson, Compass

"The Future Is Beautiful gives rise to a future we can all look forward to."

Indra Adnan, Soft Power Network

"We're told all the time that society has never been more apathetic; that rich, poor, young and old have given up on changing the world in which they live. This book and the wisdom it contains show why that's not true. The future we choose is a future we must fight for. By inspiring each other, we make it all the easier."

Will Straw, Institute for Public Policy Research

"In the pages of this book lurk some wickedly positive futures that would leave a world fit for our future generations."

Halina Ward, Foundation for Democracy and Sustainable Development

"It is rare that someone writes a book with passion where the effort is aimed not at knowing the answers but understanding the question. We live in a world that has fractured intimacies yet ever-growing digital closeness, where ideas about how we want to live are undermined by notions of wealth, consumption and the measurability of happiness. Don Quixote would have wept. This marvellous book is at once a challenge for us to try to describe the sunny uplands we wish to reach as well as being a plea for a plurality in that vision. The joy to me is that shining through it all is a series of reference points called kindness, generosity and courtesy. These are the planks most of us want to stand on as we set out on this journey. I feel a new form of democracy stirring and it is exciting and vital. Go make a difference I say. Read this book and start now."

Tim Smit, The Eden Project

THE FUTURE IS BEAUTIFUL

A Collection From Think Act Vote

THINK ACT VOTE

THE FUTURE IS BEAUTIFUL : A Collection from Think Act Vote (?!X)

Published as The Future We Choose in 2012
by Amisha Ghadiali, Think Act Vote.
New Edition 2016.

All attempts have been made to include accurate information about all of the contributors and creative activists featured in this book.

Hardback, Softback and electronic editions available at
www.thefutureisbeautiful.co

Front Cover quote by Jonathan Robinson, founder of Impact Hub
Edited by Amisha Ghadiali and Gilly Rochester
Artwork and Design by Matthieu Becker
Illustration throughout the book by Kiran Patel (Illustrating Rain)
Art Direction by Joana Casaca Lemos and Ella Britton
New Edition Cover by Johanna de Mornay Davies
Foreword by James Parr
Afterword by Sam Roddick

THINK   ACT   VOTE

Published by Think Act Vote (?!X)
East London, United Kingdom
www.thefutureisbeautiful.co

connect@thefutureisbeautiful.co
www.facebook.com/thinkactvote
www.twitter.com/thinkactvote
www.pinterest.com/thinkactvote
www.instagram.com/thefutureisbeautiful
#TheFutureIsBeautiful

The Future I Choose is the future I never could have imagined before each one of you opened my eyes.

Paul Hilder

Contents

A Note for this Edition

What struck me during the process of creating this book was how beautiful people are. The visions, inspirations and actions shared in these pages are the makings of a beautiful future.

The future is beautiful because the human spirit is beautiful.

Despite the challenges we face as a global community, or the pressures that we meet in our daily lives, when we stop and dare to dream, to ask ourselves the big questions and to share what we are already doing, we create the future that we wish to wake up for.

Our time here is precious. It's easy to forget. When we connect to our hearts and minds, and what unites us, our innate goodness and beauty, we find so much possibility, so much opportunity.

This is the revolution.
It's happening right now.
It's to be found in the day to day moments of our lives.

When we encounter it we feel more alive.

You don't have to be anything that you are not already.

Find your voice. Speak your truth. Embody your values.

Let this book be your guide, let it illuminate your soul where it may have grown dim or tired. Let the spark of joy, light and hope that each of these contributions holds inspire you.

Let your imagination run wild. Create the future.

We are the Future.

Amisha Ghadiali

Foreword

Before you flick through this book and slip into a reverie inspired
by the splendid ponderings contained within, imagine for a second that
you are a future historian from 200 years hence scrutinizing a unique
portrait of our time.

As a historian, you will know that the first years of the second decade of
the 21st Century were a period of profound flux. This in particular was
the moment when Western Civilization blinked and the world changed.
As you leaf through the musings of those long gone, buried in quaint
references to obsolete technology, you begin to feel the character of
the time - a period where, despite unprecedented challenges, there was
still an underlying belief in the power of the human spirit.

Some of the contributions, of course, seem hopelessly optimistic
to 23rd Century eyes. However, some echo through the aeons as being
precise prognostications of how the future unfolded. What's more,
buried in the thoughts of those 21st century citizens are the whispers
of the world that still could be.

This book is a unique and extraordinary time capsule of the here
and now. As you read through it, take a breath to reflect on how this
moment will be judged by our ancestors. Did we live up to the promise
of our oratory or did we stumble when the going got tough? Will future
historians lament our lip service or did we succeed in laying down
the foundations of a fair and prosperous future?

Did we merely create a better present for ourselves...
or did we choose the future?

James Parr

Introduction

Think Act Vote: A personal and collective journey

How many of us ever stop to imagine the world we want to live in, or consider how our actions can help to create it?

In some ways many of the ideologies running our world systems have failed, but there is no other belief system that has enough strength behind it. Yet amongst us we have a plethora of solutions and ideas that could lead us to a brighter future.

This book began as an idea in the pub, a few months before the 2010 UK general election. I realised that, like most of the people I spoke to, I was not excited. This was a new feeling for me. Until this point I had found elections incredibly engaging. Democracy excited me, because it represented the principle that the ideas we each have can create a direct impact on our lives and our world.

Over the past twenty years, I have seen a shift in the way that we express our values and our politics. I have seen how the rise of consumerism has changed how we express our identities, and at the same time how our identification with traditional politics has declined. What is interesting is observing this growing over the past decade, and traditional politics almost disappearing from contemporary culture.

In the UK today, less than one per cent of the electorate belongs to a political party. So how are the other ninety-nine per cent expressing their values and shaping their future lives and communities?

Like the majority, I am not a member of a political party, although I have spent many weekends at political conferences trying to be part of that conversation. The one per cent speak a very particular language, and it is one that many people I know find intimidating, aggressive or disingenuous. When you think about what an election is, on a simple level it is an opportunity for each of us to express our view on the future we choose. But elections are not so frequent and democracy has to mean more than putting an X on a ballot paper. So where is the conversation for the other ninety-nine per cent?

In the run up to the 2010 general election, instead of asking people to vote in the traditional sense, I asked them to vote by sharing their vision of the future that they choose. As we travelled to various events, the Think Act Vote ballot box created thousands of conversations, and our online community grew. As the election approached, it became clear to me that we were not suffering from apathy, but a collective frustration at the challenge of trying to share the future we choose within the current political system.

This collective frustration was expressed to us in many different ways. Some people complained about the unfairness of our voting system and the dominance of two or three political parties. Others pointed to the unrepresentative make-up of Parliament, with its narrow range of socio-economic backgrounds, sexualities and experiences. Many were concerned that the biggest issues facing us, such as sustainable development and economic prosperity, don't fit neatly into electoral cycles, which prevents us from building long-term solutions. Discomfort was shared about some of the ways the UK interacts with other countries at a time when we are all reliant on each other. And we lost count of how many times we heard people say "I don't do politics" and "it doesn't matter what I think."

Yet it was obvious to us that even those people who thought their ideas didn't matter still had visions of the future that they wanted to share. We wondered how we might capture these solutions from people who are not part of the "political class", and create a more universal language for talking about our political ideals.

Our solution was 'The Futures Interviews', and this book. We wanted to create a space for people to express themselves politically in their own language. We wanted to know the songs that had shaped people, the places they found inspiration online, as well as how we could all help create the future they choose. We were interested in how culture, science and history influenced what we desire in the world.

It was important to us to create an open place where different types of people could answer the same questions, allowing us to listen better to one another. We wanted there to be a space for people to think globally, but answer individually. We tried to go beyond words, inviting people to visualise their futures in design competitions, photobooths, and the Futures Illustrations here in this book. Think Act Vote became a radical think tank, open to anyone no matter what age, background, ethnicity, religion, sex, nationality or occupation, to contribute ideas and share personal stories to shape a brighter future.

At first I wanted the contributors of this book to form an accurate representation of the UK electorate today. Later I wanted it to feature someone from every country in the world. What I discovered quite quickly though was that these questions can be difficult to answer. They are big, and deep, and require you to commit your values to paper and to select what you think is important from all the billions of ideas in the world and moments in history. So instead I decided to let the interviews grow organically, and that anyone who was brave enough to share themselves could be in the book. I reached out to people that I knew and I met, and let the online community and social media do the rest. The majority of the contributors are living in the UK, but some have come via the United States, Kenya, India, Brazil, China, Lebanon, Lithuania and many more countries. Care has also been taken to ensure that the contributors to this project are intergenerational. Of course, this is just the start. I realise that the people in this book are all those with easy access to the internet. None of the contributors in this edition are part of the near half of the world's population living on less than $2 a day.

Rather than representing a particular group of people, this book has become an invitation to you to answer these questions in your own time, and to encourage the people that you respect to do it too. Through the process of taking part in our Futures Interviews, we invite you to reflect on what it is that you really believe in, and to articulate your core values. I want to thank all the contributors for thinking deeply about these questions, for sharing so much of themselves, and for taking a stand for what they believe in.

Reading all the interviews together, what has become clear is that there is no meaningful way to compare our individual visions. Each one comes from a thoughtful and personal place. Whether the answers come from a young student, a well-known creative figure, or an unemployed refugee, each answer teaches us something new, and asks us to look at things differently. It is perhaps revealing though that in all the many suggestions for creating the future we choose, only one person suggested joining a political party.

If I had five minutes with every human being on this planet, these are the questions that I would ask them. We spend much of our waking lives limiting ourselves, our beliefs, our power, our dreams, our actions. But when you look though history and the present, we see that people only create change in their lives and in the world by believing that more is possible than meets the eye. We all make choices in our lives about how we spend our time, energy and money, and it is these decisions that collectively shape our world.

Let's have the courage to live by our values and learn from each other, to create the future that we choose.

Amisha Ghadiali

WHAT IS THE FUTURE
THAT YOU CHOOSE?
YOUR FUTURE IS
THE WORLD YOU WANT
TO LIVE IN.

More compassion, less fear.
More Imagination, less fundamentalism.
More art, less Botox.
More organic food, NO FAMINE.
More Reverence, less boredom
More service, less greed.
More trees, less cars.
More connection, less loneliness.
More poems, less reality television.
More hope, less cynicism.
More Love, less shame.
More Love, less fear.

Meredith Hines

The future I choose is one where every person understands the interconnectedness of everything that we do; a future where people work to live; a future which is inclusive; one where we appreciate that we depend entirely on the planet on which we live and act accordingly.

Christian Smith

Less onus will be placed on commercial success. It would be nice to live without so many of our children and young people believing self-worth exists at the end of an X-Factor audition queue.

Lucie Barât

All people have equal rights
and opportunities, are treated
and perceived equally,
and are respected and accepted
as individuals and human beings.
This is the aspiration of feminism:
an environment of tolerance,
acceptance and equality, and freedom
from exploitation. In it, all people feel
empowered to be individuals,
and to receive equal encouragement,
support and acceptance in whatever paths
in life they choose to take.

Laura Nelson

I want a future where people finally set
aside their differences and value being
kind to others instead of living lives ruled
by purely selfish motives. It would be
a happier and safer world where people
would work hard for themselves but also
others, striving to be fair and just in all
their endeavours and seeking out ways,
however small, to make a difference.

Kirstie Battson

I see a future that is one of love, enthusiasm
and respect, for our people, our planet, our cultures,
our heritage, our future and our knowledge.
A future in which everyone is encouraged to take
an interest in the world around us, and to discover
that in the acquisition of such interest, there can be
much beauty, peace and happiness. In this future
we are not victims to the desire for instant gratification,
but pupils in the lessons of patience, ownership
and experience. In this future there is no hierarchy
of citizens, but a mutual respect for all skills and talents.
In this future people are not placed on pedestals
for associations, monetary gains or for the acquisition
of fame, but for their extraordinary acts of courage,
kindness and innovation. In this future we celebrate
creative strategies, cultural diversity, and the importance
of human relationships. In this future anyone can flourish
because education and opportunities are not reserved
for the elite. There are no prejudices and no stigmas;
rather, we all work together to better ourselves,
to help those less fortunate and to inspire greater
and more accessible understanding of the beautiful
and amazing world around us.

Emily Wilkie

There is perhaps one overriding idea that shapes the kind of world that I would like to live in, and that is 'inclusion'. Not the abused variety, which confuses it with integration in which people have to conform to existing dominant values and behaviour, but a world which puts the most vulnerable at its heart, and changes accordingly. A commitment to equality demands that those who are weakest or most vulnerable are given priority, are protected and are empowered. Whether it be in the world of international trade or the local community, a level playing field is not enough. It has to be slanted in favour of those who need help. And a world structured in such a way - allowing itself to be transformed by the most vulnerable - is one in which everyone benefits.

Jonathan Bartley

I envision a future where there is no correlation between excellence and exclusivity.

Peter Gregson

I want to live in a world that does not bring tears to the eyes of millions of children everyday. I would like to be able to travel anywhere in the world and not have to find people living under cruel dictatorships; under occupation; starving, living in poverty; unable to go after what they dream of. A selfless world where people do not care more about celebrities than the starving millions; where people think 'That could have been me' and work to help the unfortunate. I want the future that is available to me to be available to anyone else who wants it. A fair, equal world.

Abrar Agil

The future I choose does not bow down to built systems. The future I choose is yet to be invented. The future I choose is not afraid. The future I choose is free.

Miguel Fernandes Ceia

We can work for a future which uses the creativity
and energy of people to find solutions to the world's
big problems, such as poverty, disease, abuse of human
rights, bad government, environmental degradation,
global warming, etc. The starting point is usually
the ideas that people have, not governments.
The next step is for people to put those ideas
into practice, and then make them work.
We call these people social entrepreneurs.
They should be encouraged, and their contribution
celebrated. This is how we are going to make
a better world.

Michael Norton

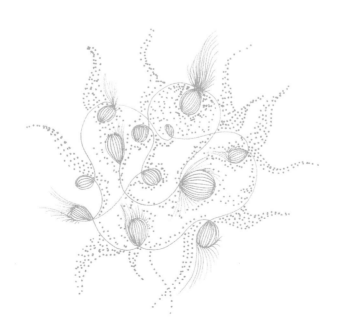

In my mind's eye and my heart's scope
I create a future that provides balance
and harmony for people and our planet.
I wish for people to receive more than
survival - rather the luxury of having
their conscience stirred, the peace
to contemplate the futures they would like
to shape, the space to discover their talents
and the resources to employ these to make
it happen.

Annegret Affolderbach

I choose a future where the western world
works in a symbiotic relationship with
the developing world, sharing the resources
in an equable way so that the West
continues to enjoy the blessings of the fruits
of the Earth, knowing that the developing
world have their opportunity to migrate
through the social stratosphere and be
the best they can possibly be.

Kriss Akabusi

The Future I Choose is a world
that believes in the beauty of truth.

Palvi Raikar

I envision a future where innovation
happens for innovation's sake, free of fear
and red tape. I choose a future where every
imagination is engaged, every voice finds
its instrument, and artists are compensated
fairly for their contributions to society.

Max Lugavere

I choose a future involving justice,
acceptance and free (eco-friendly) taxis
for the elderly ... and those in high heels.

Zara Martin

I envision a world where children can
grow and live healthily and happily,
regardless of where they are born.

Emily Renny

In the future I choose, creative thought and action is truly respected, and schooling releases individual potential. I choose a future of silver linings and more varied methods of structuring society, rising up to challenge the norm.

Philippa Young

A world where we stand together for justice and what is right, where everyone is given the freedom and opportunity to dream and make those dreams a reality.

Dominic Campbell

We shall take a more balanced, considered and creative approach to life - individuals, communities and nations will take the time and care to understand one another and their differences; we shall afford nature and the environment (both immediate and wider) the respect that they deserve; where we produce cradle to cradle, and consume with more thought. In the future I choose we will 'live gently'.

Zoe Robinson

The Future I Choose is one where equality is a deeply and intuitively held assumption in every person; a world where a person's value is not defined by their place in capitalism.

Brodie Ross

One where everyone has an equal stake in society, where people appreciate nature and don't abuse it ... and milk gets delivered in glass bottles by milkmen in little white trucks.

Gareth Barnes

I choose a world where we can see what we have collectively, rather than what we don't have individually, so that we instinctively share more.

Gloria Charles

My future is multidimensional, inspirational, creative and professional. It is a timeless place where human beings are inspired to do what they love and love what they do. It is a future where apparent failings are understood as education for life, and vulnerability is an integral part of self-development, growth and success. It is a future where learning isn't limited to a classroom or where age doesn't dictate capacity for creative flourishing or life shifts. The future I choose is a new world, where people are inspired to give themselves to causes greater than themselves, to collaborate with others who inspire them, and to inspire and support those around them. The future I choose is one where no individual is made to feel inadequate or worthless, nor better or worse off than another. The future I choose is one that will inspire humans to live out their lives to their greatest potential. It is a future where human beings understand and respect their connection to all life on earth. The future I choose is personal, global, collaborative and creative. It has an infinite perspective with a new personal reality.

Kate Andrews

We will harness the exponential progress of emerging technologies to address humanity's grand challenges. Our brains evolved in a world that was linear and local and now we live in world that is global and exponential. It means that a person with a cell phone in Africa today has better communication access than the US president did 15 years ago. David Pearce, who wrote 'The Hedonistic Imperative', speaks of "paradise engineering"... It means we use technology as the means to bring into being our spoken intent. We do create the world, and we just need to get better at it.

Jason Silva

The future I choose is one where creativity reigns supreme. Where dull, black-and-white living makes way for full colour HD ideas and community.

Jeremy Dillon

In the future that I choose, the majority of people are engaged in work that's actively in pursuit of their passions, so that love is the daily experience it's designed to be. A world where people free themselves from external expectations and conformity and assert their rights, needs and standards. A world where people take their time so that all decisions and actions are considered and conscious (as opposed to simply convenient for the short-term). In such a world, where we concentrate on the health, wellbeing and growth of our individual selves, it's inevitable that this kind of consideration will extend through to how we interact with others and the relationship we have with our environment.

Lulu Kitololo

Political engagement won't just be a buzzword. I want a future where voters are given real responsibilities (but also take them seriously), and aren't treated like idiots. This world would have fewer politicians, and they'd treat politics not as a vocation but as a public service. We'd give them the chance to be open and transparent about their convictions, ideologies and misgivings, and we'd care a little bit more about things that didn't directly affect us. This is all essentially a world where there's a realisation that integrity and frankness makes for the best politics, but also that we ought to be more in control of our lives and, by extension, our destinies.

Jag Singh

Artists and creatives are able to voice their own opinions, have free thought, individuality, and make works of art without being suppressed in any way.

Jo Cheung

It is fully transparent.
I'm not sure what sort of shape it should take, but I'd love to be able, in an instant, to know everything about a product: where it comes from, its history, how it has been made, by who and in which conditions.

Aurélie Dumont

Not a singular utopia, but a world that is more free from oppression, inequality and hierarchy, with a population more free to follow creative and individual pursuits, and with the current impending dangers of nuclear, climate and capitalistic destruction lessened.

Musab Younis

I envisage a generous future: one where people recognise and express their interdependence at every level, as part of a co-creative planetary community authentically embedded within our various ecosystems. And it all begins with me: I have to walk the talk...

Pete Yeo

The future I choose is one without prejudice and immorality. People from different ethnic and social backgrounds will not have labels assigned to them for the rest of their lives; there will be no parts of the country where certain communities are expected to live in worse conditions than others. There will be a national network of schools which are all of a sound standard that, regardless of where the child lives or the situation of their parents, he/she will still be exposed to the same opportunities. Also, women will be earning as much as men and be regarded and treated as equals in all walks of life.

Lina Jovasaite

One of inclusion, coherence, diversity and community values between people, both globally and locally.

Josie Nicholson

Policy makers and citizens will work together in order to create conditions for social justice, to give everyone the opportunity to improve their quality of life. And this can happen only when we all understand that the constructive energy of society relies on the power of human creativity and imagination. Not in the blind accumulation of money.

Maria Teresa Sette

We give all we can and take only what we need.

Rory Costello

I choose a world where citizens are encouraged to think deeply about their purpose and ethical duty. Where humans are encouraged to act in "good faith" as opposed to "bad faith", and personal integrity is a sacred value. Where institutions treat people as ends in themselves rather than means toward ends. Cooperatives are the dominant type of economic institution. The maximization of societal happiness is recognized as the ultimate goal.

Christian Flores Carignan

A utopian society may be seen as a fantasy but aspiration towards a more democratic and just society is a hope that can never be discarded. I want to live in a world where the chasm between the rich and poor is narrower, and where the most powerful countries take responsibility and help the less fortunate countries in more meaningful ways - both economically, in trade, and in their engagement with human rights.

Tizane Navea-Rogers

I see a world in which we treat each other with respect, regardless of race, ethnicity, gender, skin colour, religion etc. It is one where we are interested in enriching our own lives as well as others', and where we are not simply being titillated by celebrity gossip or how 'sexy' we look to the opposite gender. It is one where people are educated, not just in an academic sense but in a social sense – a world where prejudices and stereotypes are overcome; a future where we can think for ourselves and not be led by certain media outlets into believing untruths.

Iram Ramzan

I choose the potential of a future for everyone. There are many in our societies and across the world who have no opportunities, no power, no wealth, little education and support and therefore have no way to make a better life. For them life is survival, the future isn't even on the agenda. Being able to discuss what the future holds is the privilege of the wealthy and empowered.

Chris Arnold

Environmental preservation will be on an equal footing with the economy in terms of importance for our future. And the work/life balance will be far more sanely proportioned.

Alistair Humphreys

Greater equality of opportunity from the earliest age.

Dan Snow

I choose a future where the word waste ceases to exist in our dictionaries.

Shibin Vasudevan

I would love to see a future
of more sharing,
less owning,
more creating,
less consuming,
more understanding
and less judging.
Oh and more cake
and more tea.

Anila Babla

I choose a society that is based on empathy. Where previous barriers to human compassion no longer hold sway. Where we all recognise the responsibility in each of us to seek the understanding of and respect for all walks of life, including the animal kingdom and our biosphere. Where freedom of culture would be protected - by institutions built by the efforts of innovative and collaborative individuals with acknowledgement of how the increasing connectivity the world must allow for the flourishing of local culture. A future economy that fuels itself by ethical and sustainable trading, where countries are no longer driven to impose low wages or cash-crop export farming to ensure their piece of the global market. In this future, values inherent to all of humanity - dignity, self-sustenance and association – are woven through our business practices, politics and legal systems, as well as in our civil engagement.

Christina Rebel

A world that is driven by love and respect, not fear and greed: we'll all be on the same side and working together in support of each other. We'll be using our creative energy to solve the world's problems and we'll be having fun whilst we're doing it. The future I choose is one where it is sexy and cool to care about the planet and its people. The future I choose is open, sustainable and collaborative. It's one where we know our values and live by them, where what we do takes into account the future, the past and the present. It's one where we are not afraid to share what's important to us, and the world that we want to create, and can then work together with trust and respect. In the future I choose we are free to do the right thing without fear of repercussions, and our actions take the ways in which they will affect others into account.

Amisha Ghadiali

Individuals and communities will be empowered to act together for the greater planetary good.

Amelia Gregory

No borders, no boundaries, no religion, no reason for war and anger. The future I'd choose would be one of world peace and cooperation. Water, food and good health for all, and a global environmental policy that ensures these for all generations to come.

Luke Tucker

Africa does not rely on aid but has systems and strategies in place to support and grow their own economies and people.
As much as businesses create employment and opportunities for people, the real change will come when governments create long-term strategies for good governance and development.
With this in place, the term 'Trade not Aid' can really come into play. People then have the freedom and support to be entrepreneurial and create trade, employment and development within their own country.

Joanna Maiden

My choice is built on the theory that the future is actually now, so living the moment with balance and devotion is a recurrent mantra. No 3rd or 1st world. No 2nd or 1st class.

Joao Machado

The ways in which we are interconnected will be more visible, so that empathy can thrive and a sense of collective responsibility and compassion cannot be ignored. It's a future where we can really link up with each other in very human ways; love would be at the centre of that. It is a world where we look after one another, not through services, but through human connection; people will be creating together, sharing together, solving problems together, overcoming adversity together, believing in one another, trusting one another. A future where people are able to see possibility, have hope and cultivate what they are talented at. If we were all able to do that then I believe so many other things would just fall into place.

Cassie Robinson

The future I choose is the same as that which millions of people around the world have chosen - one based on the words of Martin Luther King, Grace Lee Boggs and Billy Bragg. One where people are judged based on the content of their character, not on the colour of their skin, their gender, sexuality, or ability.
One where people have equal opportunity and equal protection; where we harness the power of our sun and wind to give us energy, rather than digging ever deeper into the earth and endangering the health of our families and communities.
One where we are free.

Hanna Thomas

A socially egalitarian world, where people are judged equally, regardless of their work, salary or family set-up. One in which religion and gender and sexuality and language are the starting points for building a collective understanding of humanity, rather than the sources of hatred and struggle.

One in which the social construct of race is torn down.

One in which education is both local and worldly, and allows children to think for themselves.

One in which jobs are respected and rewarded for being the ones with the most positive social and environmental impact. In short: the future I choose is one in which everyone is given an equal opportunity to flourish and to thrive.

Eugenie Teasley

I choose a future focussing on equality of opportunity but also celebration of difference. The concept of 'normality' as a societal or personal aspiration is one of the most destructive concepts we have. The exclusion of the 'other' and labelling of a person as strange, deficient or unworthy promotes fear, decimates self-esteem and leads ultimately to unhappiness.

We see the ramifications of social exclusion and marginalization in our prison system and mental hospitals. The future I choose embodies 'Equality of Opportunity', where no one is excluded from trying - by virtue of difference of gender, sexuality, creed, accent, birthplace, race or age; a level playing field where people are encouraged to spread their talents across a mixture of fields (creative, charitable, familial, financial); and a future where we work together to protect dignity - because human development is dependent upon confidence. A future where we put our money where our mouth is - where the most important not the most glamorous jobs in our society receive the best rewards. I choose a future where the gilded butterflies of celebrity are not elevated over roles of substance or utility at the expense of our children's aspiration or self-esteem.

Karis McLarty

One where the sustainable thing is the easiest thing to do - so, for example, more people get out of their cars and have fun whizzing around on bicycles.

Vicky Murray

I hope for a time when young people are as keen to vote for politicians as they are to vote for X-factor contestants.

Chris Lonie

I want a world where people take responsibility not only for their actions but also for the appearance of where they live - I want people to look after their neighbourhood, keep it clean and encourage others to do so too. I don't want people to say "It's the Council's job" or "I'm not picking up litter that's been dropped by other people". I want everyone to say "I am going to keep my neighbourhood clean and tidy, encourage my friends and neighbours to join me in doing so", and achieve a much cleaner, happier and safer community in the process.

George Monck

I choose a future where we are not just consumers, but creativists. At the moment, the identity that people are given in society is as consumers. Consumers are passive. If we are to move to a more sustainable future, we need an alternative identity that we can take on. Creativists are active. Creativists connect, create and act. And creativists choose the future they want!

Olivia Sprinkel

I choose jungles filled with wild animals and a sea dense with fish and thriving reefs, and butterflies and bees that don't die out, and clean air to breathe.

Tyler Wetherall

The barriers between nature and societies are blurred; where we all think of ourselves as environmentalists, as the environment is our umbilical cord for life; and therefore a world where we fulfil our role as caretakers of the planet.

Jo Royle

There'd be a focus on happiness and well-being, which leads to a conscious life. A future where it's about more than just more money. Where it is about respect for each other and our environment and resources. Altruism is held in higher regard than egoism. It's great to give and you get so much in return. We are a social species.

Arjan Hofmann

One where putting the environment first is a reflex.

James Parr

I choose a healthier future. Organic, free range and natural foods are more accessible. The future is greener in everything we do, choose, create, see and live in. We are on each other's side, we inspire each other and help each other. The future I choose is about paying it forward!

Vicky Fallon

I want to live in a place where, when someone says 'green', it no longer makes others think "Oh, fuck off, you hippy". It's a place where people respect the fact we need to leave an environmental legacy for future generations; where Western society steps out of its commercialised bubble and reconnects with the land it originally came from. We will all live with respect for our belongings, grow our own veg, be grateful for what we have - and do it all with community spirit.

Ellie Good

I want a world where everyone has a chance to gain
fulfilment in their daily lives. I choose a future where
the skills that have been acquired through time are kept
alive, where people use their raw talents to trade
and where we do not surrender to a purely virtual age.
The future I choose enables sustainability and living
off the land we live on instead of exploiting others
and sending products all over the globe. My future
is culturally vibrant and supportive without twisted
corruption and greed. Most of all, the future I choose
ensures people have self-awareness and individual
thought that does not mean they continue under
the assumption that somebody else will do something
about issues they ignore. Most of all, the future I choose
means that others choose too, and act, instead of
the collective apathy that appears to reign.

Hester Russell

The future that I choose is one of balance, harmony, and great thought and attention to detail. In the fashion and design industry there is always a rush to get on to the next new 'trend', 'season', 'style' or 'look' and, as fun as this can be, there is no real longevity or sustainability to this. The future that I choose is based on considering my actions carefully and hoping that others will follow suit and do the same. Changing my perceptions from within, in order to create in a realistic and organic way, will hopefully influence others to do the same. I would especially like to see the growth and resurrection of old craft techniques, less mass production and more thought being put into our consumables, so that they become less throwaway. Building responsibility towards our own objects and creating relationships with them means that more thought goes into the purchasing process. To me, the future lies in the hands of the consumers and the public. People don't realize quite how much power they have to change things. Yet.

Rachel Holland

I see a world based on honesty,
transparency and good intentions.
It is a place where we can trust in those
around us to give us the entire story.
Also, it is a place in which we each realize
that by thinking through our individual
processes of creating our own story,
we can positively affect people
and the planet along the way.
It is a thoughtful place, where through
conscious actions we can treat people
and the planet with respect.

Kestrel Jenkins

I want a world where people can safely
express their opinions and strive to reach
their goals in this life, without suppression,
persecution or fear. To finally accept
that each individual has got a voice
to communicate their views, whether
it be verbally, written or visually.
No one's voice should ever be suppressed.

June Chanpoomidole

The future I choose is fitter, healthier,
happier, less greedy, more liveable,
more equal and beautifully designed.

Wayne Hemingway

I want to see a society in which we all value
social justice as much as capital.

Tim Adey

The future I choose is essentially what I wrote in my book 'Grow' a few years ago; it's written from a woman's perspective and called 'shaping the future': "As women we are traditionally the caretakers of our culture; our responsibility is to understand and somehow make sure that changes that are happening in our world preserve the basic humanity in us all. By connecting with the principles of the sacred feminine, such as those found in ancient matriarchal civilizations, the more nurturing society can evolve. One that abhors violence, advocates such values as justice, compassion and love, and raises its children to reach their full potential as human beings. If we are talking about getting rid of the old, outdated, patriarchal ways of running the world then it's essential to present a pragmatic vision of what we want to replace it with.

We need an overall blueprint of what a new world based on principles of the sacred feminine would look like and how it would work. The primary foundation for a world is cooperation. First and foremost is cooperation between male and female. As women we know that the best and most efficient way to get things done is to work together. And that means living and working with men in harmonious coexistence, valuing the perspectives and strengths of both sexes and creating a higher quality of life for all. It must also be a world of cooperation between business and community, human beings and the planet, national governments and NGOs, young and old, spirituality and science and our inner and outer selves."

Lynne Franks

A world where each person is taught to love themselves as the basis of living a happy life. Whether a person comes from the most dire upbringing or most desperate financial circumstances, truly believing that we are each worthy of living a good life is the cornerstone to creating a collectively happier planet. People who love themselves find it easy to love others – and the gifts of that are both transformative and boundless.

Kellee Rich

One where people understand the depth behind the things they say and the true power of the spoken word. A joke to one person is racism and discrimination to another. People need to be educated so that we can all be equals. Differences are only as important as you make them.

Evie Stretch

Profit is not the bottom line and our value as people is not defined by the objects we own, but how we treat each other and the world around us.

Laura Billings

The Future I Choose is where we do not rely on materialism for happiness. Where we enjoy life without the need to always keep up with the latest fashion - whether it be clothing, gadgets or furniture for our homes. I choose a future where we value every possession and think carefully before buying, considering the impact on the environment and whether everyone involved in the supply chain has been treated with the respect that they deserve.

Ceri Heathcote

I choose a future where everything is fairer – the distribution of power, of resources, of respect. I'd also like an environmentally-sound hover board please.

Rick Edwards

I choose a world built on values of collaboration and altruism, a future where we respect people and the planet in equal measures. The future I choose doesn't ignore failures but honestly embraces them as important agents for positive change. The future I choose places higher value over long-term sustainability rather than short-term gains. The future I choose to build is one that is more promising, more just and more beautiful than what came before.

Sarah Ditty

Everybody's skills will be nurtured so that they want to contribute to society. In this future, people will find dignity in what they do and be filled with a sense of purpose.

Rhea Babla

Gender, age, sexual orientation or religion do not cause barriers between people, or to their harmony or their progression in life. It is a world where our kids are free to play on the streets and where you could put your handbag on the floor without worrying about it. A world where leaders of our countries work together to create a better world. A world where people care about our planet and the beauty around us. It is a world where politics are transparent and the future is steered as much by the people as it is by the egos of those in power. I choose a world of peace and harmony, where people love their neighbour, and greed and the desire to hurt others is not part of anyone's DNA.

Vanessa Vallely

Where we're all happy in our own skins, where we can live our lives channelling our energy into delivering to our highest potential. The future I choose is as part of a community which encourages us to live out our dreams, bringing the salt (creativity, commerce, integrity) and light (knowledge, joy, goodness) to the people, businesses and communities we impact on, operate with and live in. The future I choose is a world living as sustainably as is possible, where economic growth and commercial trading structures deliver the chance to receive a fair wage and meaningful work for individuals and communities. The future I choose is in a world where informed, creative and sustainable design, manufacturing and craft are commonplace.

Alex Smith

The Future I Choose is a Glastopolitics, where groups can work together where they feel most comfortable, whether that's on the fringes or on the main stage.

Noel Hatch

It's creative, connected, cultured, with less consumption and waste.

David Hawksworth

A world with fewer shoes and more views on things that matter and have beauty.

Louie Louie Herbert

All creatures and ecologies will be respected
and nurtured; resources are fairly and carefully used.
Creativity and innovation is valued, and greed
and destruction non-existent. Where children
can play outdoors; where birds and bees flourish.
A place where we have more time to spend
with friends and family; where home life and work life
is designed to be zero waste and resourceful;
full of music and dancing. Where limits to our
imaginations do not exist. Where environmental
and social care is a core belief. Where all have
opportunities and can achieve the highest order
of their being.

Lucy Gilliam

In the future I choose, people from every corner
of the globe can determine their own future. A future
that is not determined by the power we hold
or the amount of weapons we own. Where children
carry pencils and pens rather than guns and pistols.
Where religion has no meaning other than faith,
and governments see past their own greed. I choose
a future that would not require others to wish
for what their own future was like, but to have
equal opportunities to see it happen.

Dina Yunis

I choose a future marked by climate justice in the developed world and social justice in the developing world.

Richard Leyland

A world without waste; a future that has more balance, where we in the privileged parts of the world do not squander the resources which belong to all, and can empower more awareness in everyday actions, such as use of water.

Sandy Black

We'll be reacquainted with the politics of equality and want to get involved. We'll no longer be satiated with cheap goods made on the back of exploited workers in the developing world, trapped in poverty. There are lots of progressive pockets like this already; we just need to roll it out!

Lucy Siegle

A world that is eco-friendly, where recycling becomes a priority in every household!

Daisy de Villeneuve

All our resources and energy will be renewable and sustainable: by investing in clean and truly renewable technology and ways of working, we all have the capacity to envision and participate in a less doom-ridden future. I look forward to this future where ownership wars for finite resources are left behind, making way for more positive developments in human culture.

Jocelyn Whipple

I have a vision of a future where people refuse to accommodate injustice, and war will be universally considered as senseless; a future where there will be an open dialogue between all peoples from all nations to work towards a future where peace is not just an option but the only way forward.

Kav Sidhu

Creative talent and resources will be utilised to close the widening gap between the rich and the poor. Diversity transcends from a tick box and unites people in celebrating difference. Young and old are given equality of opportunity and social capital is this and next season's new trend. It is a time where being great and celebrating the success of those from tomorrow is embraced, enjoyed and unleashed. The future I choose is one where we say I am proud to be a part of that.

Justice Williams

One where we've met the needs of today whilst enhancing the ability of everyone to meet their needs tomorrow.

Solitaire Townsend

A future where we realise the positive impact we can have on the people and the world around us through our daily decisions and actions. It's 'us and us' not 'us and them'. It's an interconnected, transparent, collaborative, empathic and fun future.

Henry Hicks

The Future I Choose is a world in which no one's choices of things to do or buy are blindly determined by others. A world where our decisions are open and the impacts transparent, so we can begin to really see how each of us affects other people and the planet. A world of empathy, not apathy.

Jessi Baker

People will be happy from within - this expresses itself in healthy and beautiful habits: from the way that people eat to the way they relate to others.

Sarah Lloyd-Hughes

The future I choose is shiny, happy and evenly distributed.

Lucy Shea

We are one, we are all involved in creating the future.

Ada Zanditon

Young people are inspired, not apathetic and cynical, and are believers in their power to cause positive and political reform.

Jameela Oberma

It's a world in which every person can fulfil their potential without being bounded by race, class, gender or geography. That means removing more than physical constraints – it involves removing psychological ones too. You can have all the skill and luck and resources in the world, but if you don't have faith you'll get to your destination, you'll never even set off. I want everyone to choose their own future, and to believe they can get there.

Rowenna Davis

It is not a future that we can buy, vote for, or are given, but is the one that you and I will MAKE.

Indy Johar

I choose a future where we have the dictionary definition of democracy, government by the people, for the people, and tolerance of minority views.

Katharine Hamnett

What I would choose for tomorrow is a today in which we all dare to dream bigger, undertake greater adventures, tell richer stories and strive to be more curious - thereby collectively solving the issues that we know the future will hold.

David de Rothschild

The Future I Choose is green.
Not just a colour.
Not just a political party.
Not just a term for naivety!
It's a philosophy and a creative, experimental, cutting edge,
super-sexy approach to life and lifestyle that is what the 21st
century will be all about. Where we live, how we work together,
how we get around, what we eat, where it grows, what fuels
our fires, warms our hearts and inspires our minds – all are
up for grabs...we're beginning to realise consuming ever vaster
quantities of 'stuff' ain't making us happier (and we certainly
can't eat money), and that unequal societies make us sick –
physically and mentally. The future I choose is in tune
with the earth beneath our feet, recognises us as people,
not just consumers, and celebrates our collective potential
to do the right thing. And I think we might even get there!

Ed Gillespie

I see a world of harmonised rhythm, pattern and unity.
By reconnecting to our true roots in nature we can unveil
the systematic patterns, the hidden data, the building blocks
of the universe. By designing in harmony and response
to our environment and this deeper understanding,
we can complement and enhance nature's evolution.
By embracing the notion of 'open source' in every area
of our lives we can move away from the protectionist
mentality of the past into an open, sharing, balanced
evolutionary world of optimism, honesty and success!

Evan Grant

The struggles of those who came before us will not be not in vain. Nothing is ever forgotten and we would do well to remember that...

Kirstin Knox

A place where 1 and 1 actually makes 11. An environment where free-thinking radicals share successes and failures, co-create, motivate, inspire and support. A world that breathes energy and serenity at the same time. That place where people are willing to listen and act.

Mariangela De Lorenzo

The future I choose is a Free World. With the internet and the global crash, it seems clear now that our fates are intertwined, our futures interdependent, our liberty interconnected and our peace or war inseparable. So if your future is my future and my future your future, I say we ought both to be free. Free to laugh, free to love, free to worship and free to think, say and be as we wish.

Sean Carasso

The future I choose looks like the present I live in. Where change is the only constant and where we all have a fair chance at creating our present and changing anything we'd like to see differently. A future where the present is all we need. And a future where we can all enjoy this incredible opportunity we live in, called LIFE.

Bruno Pieters

I see a rainbow at sunrise. It's the mingling of the future
you choose with the future she hopes for, and the future
they hardly dared to dream. Most of all, it's the future I never
even thought of – before each one of you opened my eyes.
It's the future we choose. Togetherness in tomorrow.
It grows from listening to each other, sharing the very best of
our impulses and insights, ear to mouth and heart to heart.
A future where we bump into each other day after day and
in the blink of an eye, there we are again, familiar faces and
new, rolling our sleeves and plunging in - up to our elbows -
together. Moulding our hopes into a richer, better future.

This future I choose is a future where my sons are grown and
strong and full of life, choosing their own shared and individual
futures, and challenging us old fools on all we left undone –
because we will never do it all. But knowing what we did do,
how we shot the rapids of our time ... it's a future where
we can still sleep deeply at night, and take the deepest of
breaths, and pause... and truly delight, together in this moment,
in the light of the clearing, the wonder of our short lives,
and the slow rebounding of the only world we share.

Paul Hilder

THINKS

?
?
?
?
?
?
?
?
?
?
?
?
?
?
?
?
?
?
?
?
?

YOUR THINK IS
SOMETHING THAT
HAS INFORMED
AND INSPIRED
THE FUTURE
THAT YOU CHOOSE.

Christian Marclay's extraordinary 24-hour video art project, "The Clock," is a re-arrangement of thousands of movie clips that accurately depict a functional clock. It dawned on me when I first saw it that not only do we live in an increasingly interconnected world, where actions taken by a person can almost instantly cause a reaction in another corner of the world, but more importantly and whether we like it or not, our lives revolve around time. We're unique individuals, so isn't it strange that we all have exactly 24 hours every day to make the most of our lives? Shouldn't that inspire us to achieve and do more?

Jag Singh

"365 Ways to Change the World" gives a big issue for each day of the year, and some little actions that can start to make a difference. Your small actions could lead on to bigger and bigger things. The important things are to (a) identify an issue you feel passionate about and want to address, (b) devise a way of addressing that issue, using your brain in a creative way to come up with a solution and (c) get started. As Lao Tzu said more than 2000 ago: "A journey of 1,000 miles begins with a single step."

Michael Norton

One of the key things that has made me realise how important a clean neighbourhood is to all of us is research carried out by Professor Jonathan Shepherd at Cardiff University. His research shows that there is a strong link between the presence of litter and not only crime but, just as corrosive, fear of crime.

George Monck

As the UN Secretary-General Kofi Annan said in 2006: "It is impossible to realise our goals while discriminating against half the human race. As study after study has taught us, there is no tool in development more effective than the empowerment of women." And I have chills... every time I read this.

Kestrel Jenkins

As a writer, my Think is inspired by the Slovenian cultural theorist and philosopher Slavoj Žižek: "Words are never 'only words'; they matter because they define the contours of what we can do."

Sarah Ditty

My Think evolves from a quote from a Chekhov story 'Gusev', a maritime story that ends with the lead character's corpse being eaten by sharks: 'The sea has neither meaning nor pity.' I believe you can simply replace the word 'sea' with 'space' - in other words Chekhov is referring to the universe or perhaps time. This bleakness, this alertness to the situation we are in I believe shocks at first, but ultimately encourages kindness and well thought-out action. Chekhov became a doctor, devoting much of his life to helping people. This story can be found in the collection 'The Steppe and Other Stories'.

Patrick Hussey

My Think is this translated lyric from an old Arabic song: "From the pain we will create victory". It goes for anything. Studying for exams is painful but it usually pays off. Getting hurt by others isn't easy but it makes you stronger and wiser. The Egyptian revolution seemed hopeless when it started out but they managed to get rid of Mubarak in the end. Patience and perseverance can and will get you anywhere you want in life.

Abrar Agil

My mentor and great friend Marcelo Yuka impressed me the first time I ever met him in Rio, Brazil, in February 2000. This man had similar ideas to mine but in the right order. He is one of the greatest musicians of his generation, a fabulous activist and relentless campaigner. In Brazil, there is so much to be done, and in other places too. From our long conversations, I realised that if we don't allow half of the population to step up and act, be confident, enabled, have a voice and be respected, we'll never get all the work done. He says: "An absurdity silences another absurdity; if you open the papers today, there will be a new absurdity that will make you forget yesterday's."

Servane Mouazan

In terms of a mental construct, I like to say that we should all live unapologetically curious, with a sense of creative entitlement, and see the wonder in everything we do. And... "be kind, for everyone you meet is fighting a hard battle." I think Plato wrote that.

Max Lugavere

I find Pierre Rabhi's life, battles and writings very inspirational. Pierre Rabhi is a French/Algerian farmer, environmentalist, philosopher and writer. He has pioneered organic farming methods and has created the "oasis in every place" concept. He fosters farming models respectful of the soils and the local communities while prioritising the accessibility to the poorest. He has been working in Africa, France and Europe on many agro-ecological projects. Now a consultant at the UN and the World Bank he invites us to think outside the infinite growth scheme and call for happy moderation. One of his books, where he intimately interlinks ecology and spirituality, has been translated into English: 'As in the Heart, So in the Earth: Reversing the Desertification of the Soul and the Soil'.

Aurélie Dumont

René Descartes once said: "I think therefore I am." I believe that 'thinking' is the ultimate act of humanity. It determines who we are. Without it we are nothing. It is for this reason that countless governments and regimes have attempted over and over again to suppress human thoughts because that is the ultimate threat to authority. Through our own thoughts we are able to take control of what determines who we are and who we wish to become. The mind is a powerful tool; if not, then why is it that those in power try so hard to control the mass's minds. With human thought comes individuality, and I believe in that individuality; and as long as individuals are capable of thinking and making their own decisions, there is some hope that one day the future I chose may be able to occur: "At any given moment you have the power to say this is not how the story is going to end (Anon)."

Dina Yunis

My Think is a homeless man I met in Norway.
He was intelligent, didn't drink but seemed helpless.
I chatted to him for a while trying to understand how
he got to this position in life. He told me he'd had
a good job, a good income, a home, family and then
one day it all fell apart. He lost his job.
At first he thought he'd get another but as the months
passed the debts grew, his confidence crumbled,
he became stressed and suffered a mild breakdown.
Finally they took his house away. His wife left him.
"Suddenly I was on the streets," he said. "No one in
the position I was in ever thinks you can fall this low
but it can happen to anyone. And once you are down
here it's like a deep well, almost impossible to climb
back up." Boy did that make me think about what
you have, and only by thinking about how we can fall
back can we consider how we go forward.

Chris Arnold

Read the article 'The New Face Of Unemployment: Young, Qualified and Crippled By Debt' on Change.org to understand what kind of future our youth is currently facing. Also the BBC News article 'Rich-poor divide wider than 40 years ago' The issue of class divide is widely debated, but is dismissed as a simple economic consequence, rather than seen as a sign of our political system's failure. I believe that the class divide is inefficiently addressed in legislation, and child poverty should be targeted more urgently. If we ignore it, we are ignoring it at our peril. The 2011 Riots in the UK are something none us want to ever see again.

Tizane Navea-Rogers

I studied Economics A-Level and had an eccentric teacher who made us sit in a freezing cold class room and talked for hours about the rich-poor divide, economics and the developing world, to wear more clothes rather than turn the heating on, to only flush the toilet when essential and drive no faster than 40-something mph because that was when your car ran at optimum efficiency. She threw books at us on the developing world, corporate social responsibility and different ways to view the world. One such book that will always stay with me is 'The Diving Bell and the Dragonfly: A Memoir of Life in Death' by Jean-Dominique Bauby. This was all over 13 years ago and was the first I'd ever heard of this stuff – she definitely ignited a fire in my belly! Thanks Vreni Oleram.

Joanna Maiden

As Aristotle said, the role of the polis is to promote the good life, for all its citizens. Government that cements its place in a society by protecting its privileges above its principles soon loses both. Society leaders are advanced privilege by the words, wallets and work of others. Businesses in this country must be ethically and sustainably sourced from the beginning to the end, and ensure that profits do not originate via violence, deception or abuse - and no blind eyes are turned because of the profits made. Corporate governance, fairness in trading practices and conditions, financial contracting, sales practices, consultancy services, tax payments, and audits – all aid equality of opportunity and human development. Our government must be unapologetic in bringing corporations which flout ethical principles to justice.

Karis McLarty

Coco Chanel said: "Fashion is made to become unfashionable." By its very nature, fashion is designed to become obsolete or unfashionable after a period of time. In a world where resources are becoming scarce and the desire for low cost clothing often leads to unethical production, it seems like madness to constantly buy things that will fade or become unfashionable in such a short amount of time. Isn't it better to look stylish and invest in high quality clothes that have been made at a lower cost to both people and the environment, and will look better and last much longer?

Ceri Heathcote

We all need to think more, and ask more questions. We need to think: Where does this come from? Is there a big carbon footprint associated with buying this item? Are the people involved in the supply chain being treated fairly and gaining a fair and just price for their goods and efforts? Are working conditions safe and fair for those people? Are unnecessary amounts of chemicals being used that not only destroy the environment but also result in long-term health issues for local floral and fauna? And the biggy: Do I really need this?

Sam Rose

I was importing parcels of Fairtrade shoes from Ethiopia. I saw a gay rights message board based in Africa, on which someone like a priest had written in to ask peoples' names so that they could be "taught a lesson". I am gay. I thought: "Why am I promoting products from a country where so many people would kill me? Why not promote human rights in those countries instead of just trade?"

John Robertson

The existence of rubbish dumps and polluting landfills stresses the importance of the need to minimize our production of waste. It doesn't make sense to continually produce packaging/containers etc. that ultimately become obsolete after only one use; if you do use it, why not recycle it and re-use it in another form? Earthships are a brilliant example of this.

Alison Day

I've been intrigued by this quote for many years: 'A man there was, though some did count him mad, the more he cast away the more he had'. John Bunyan, from 'The Pilgrim's Progress From This World To That Which Is To Come'. Put another way: the more you give, the more you get. A powerful thought! I suspect that, deep down, we all know this. And in my experience, life does work this way.

Pete Yeo

I have a picture in my head from about 30 years ago in my early twenties, playing football in my father's village with all these children, some of whom were my half brothers and sisters. Football is a uniting game.

At the end of the game, I was speaking to some of the children and somebody pointed out that this little boy was my half brother. The boy looked about 8 or 9 to me but he was actually 16. And I realised that he had less opportunity in this world than I had. And just by an accident of history being born in the United Kingdom as opposed to Nigeria, the infrastructure in this country has given me an opportunity to grow to my full stature: physically, emotionally, intellectually, psychologically. A gift I wouldn't have had, had I been born in the country of my heritage. And unfortunately that situation still exists today.

Kriss Akabusi

I think the animal whose plight has most horrified me is the tiger. According to the WWF we have lost 97% of our wild tigers this century. Now that we have almost succeeded in driving tigers to extinction in the wild through hunting, poaching and destroying its habitat - through commercial plantations and illegal logging - we are about to lose a creature whose grace, power and strength has fascinated poets and artists for centuries. The poet A. D. Hope contrasts the 'authentic roar' of the 'jungle tiger' with the 'plaintive, savage hunting cry' of the paper tigers of business and politics. He exhorts us readers to try and remain true to our ideals, even though they might 'destroy the mortal parts of you', and ignore the cry of the paper tigers. I think we need to pay less attention to paper tigers and more to jungle tigers.

Tabitha Potts

A think is the ribbon you tie on a gift. Thought comes after inspiration and vision. It's about intention, enquiring and questioning. Often people spend a lot of time on thinking about how they are different and using this as a way to market themselves. What informs the future I choose is highlighting that which is similar or universal. Even in the most disparate things, there are always interconnections if we choose to see them. I see them as different, offering opportunities for learning.

Lauren Craig

Brene Browne's work about vulnerability is central to my hopes for the future. Without creating space for vulnerability we keep parts of us closed off from connecting with others, with the world. By being open, which can feel vulnerable at times, we open ourselves up to new experiences, to other views, to new possibilities. By showing our vulnerabilities we let others in, we make space for connecting more widely, more deeply, more meaningfully. We expose ourselves as being fully human.

Cassie Robinson

I observe those around me: watching the news, at work, travelling and commuting. Not only do I observe but I also listen. Especially during these recent years I listen to these stories: "I wish I had tried another career," "I could've have done so much better," "What if I'd done this," "I want to leave but I can't" etc. . It's the negativity, fear and doubt that halt you in your tracks. I totally empathise because I can relate to this. This cycle of doubt can turn into bitterness and self hate; can manifest itself into violence or a defeated existence. A simple act of kindness and compassion doesn't cost a thing; ultimately it can make someone's bad day into a good one. I think if compassion and humility were at the forefront of people's minds, it would change the way we interact.

June Chanpoomidole

I have always been fond of this particular quote from John Steinbeck's A Winter of Discomfort: "No man really knows about other human beings. The best he can do is to suppose that they are like himself." It is true that we must hope that others would act the same as us in terms of kindness and consideration, yet unfortunately this is not always the case. It would be great if we could have more confidence in our fellow man and if there was more trust and compassion in our society. This is something I hope we can work towards.

Kirstie Battson

I think the solutions to the biggest problems faced by people and the planet are to be found in nature. The next time you find yourself confronted with a problem look for ways in which nature has solved it.
For example, if you want to find a way to be more water efficient, research how species in deserts source and store water.

Melissa Sterry

....

People: their daily joy, their daily grind, their daily courage & their daily tragedy. The knowledge that a world can change when we unite. I grew up in East Germany within the confinements of The Wall. I spent my childhood standing on tiptoes trying to peak over the edges and searching for the cracks that would let in the light. I was there when The Wall came down. It was a powerful time. My people made it topple. They united, took their courage to the streets, made their voices heard. There were a few weeks after the event when nothing was set in stone – politics, education, supermarket shelves: all was in suspense. It equipped me with feelings of what I can only describe as freedom, hope and fearlessness for my future. In essence, it provided the consciousness that I could make it happen my way.

Annegret Affolderbach

....

A Think that has inspired me to create this future is a quote from Mother Teresa "There is no key to happiness, the door is always open."

Bruno Pieters

....

One of the quotes that inspires me is: 'My art is my life and my life is my art' (Unknown). This sums up how I like to go about life. With great care, great beauty and responsibility. As I child I was taught by artists Lizzie Organ and Eugene Fisk and they instilled in me a belief that although my art was different to everyone else's, it was okay to be different. Elizabeth practised 'the art of living' and this joie de vivre and self-expression influenced me into my adult life, making me realize that anything could be created, breathed and lived.

Rachel Holland

My Think is any random act of kindness I have
encountered. Probably the most recent one was during
a particularly monsoon-like deluge of rain.
As per usual, I was rather badly dressed
for an occasion such as this, dressed in a t-shirt
and sporting my shades. No umbrella either,
(in my defence, it looked sunny when I stepped out),
so I was getting very drenched, looking sorry
for myself, hiding under an equally sad tree.
Somebody came out of the house opposite, invited me
in and even gave me a lift back to my home.
Moments like that remind us that we are more than
a sum of our parts when we act cooperatively.
We are a better species than a glance at the morning
papers would lead you to believe.

Darrell Goodliffe

....

Slowing down I gain perspective of a new day

Slowing down I gain perspective of a new day
To understand that life does not exist for us
Is a revelation of ego to let go of control
We strive to gain this control each day losing our ideal
We are a part of life as we are of nature
The elongating desire of moulding life in our hands is fruitless
If we embrace life we embrace a soulful connection to the now
Being in tune with life keeps the natural at bay
One is not lost in the meaningless importances that attempt to grab us
A virtuous cause, a damsel in distress, a war of roses all were once the
Driving force of culture
And now personal advancement, materialism and fame take place of any
Character driven cause
The charities of today are even driven by socialites of repetition
Our society hungers for substance and meaning
And yet we keep producing a plastic world made in China.

....

Jeff Garner

My Think is 'Wild Geese' by Mary Oliver. I think too often poetry is condemned as 'boring' or 'irrelevant'. For me poetry, as with all literature, has played a fundamental part in my happiness and development. It has taught me the pleasure and importance of always engaging with new experiences, thoughts and perceptions. Literature facilitates constant discovery and, importantly, inspires new interest, which encourages greater understanding and a broader horizon. For me, much of the beauty in poetry can be found by letting the images resonate without too much focus on the desired intent or meaning.

Emily Wilkie

A book that was influential in developing my thinking was Erich Fromm's 'The Sane Society'. He was a psychoanalyst and social philosopher, and wrote The Sane Society in the 1950s – identifying even then how consumerism was having a negative effect on our society and who we are as human beings. He captures the struggle between creating and consuming, and how in creating we can transcend ourselves. "Man—man and woman— can create by planting seeds, by producing material objects, by creating art, by creating ideas, by loving one another. In the act of creation man transcends himself as a creature, raises himself beyond the passivity and accidentalness of his existence into the realm of purposefulness and freedom …".

Olivia Sprinkel

I love Miroslav Holub's poem 'The Door' and the idea that change in itself involves taking chances and that change has positive consequences. Holub expresses change as an individual's commitment to embrace new opportunities presented to them, leading to a new perspective of life. The door, being the central metaphor of the poem, represents a barrier, which holds us back from instigating a change.

Anila Babla

The Think that inspired me is definitely the Ghandi quote: "Be the change you wish to see." I'm forever looking at myself and asking: "Am I living my life that way?". We all have preconceived ideas and judgements that don't actually serve us.

June Sarpong

I have always been moved by the work of Ben Okri. In 2011 he published a book called 'A Time For New Dreams' which is a collection of poems, essays and thoughts. The work focuses on the future that awaits us, and asks profound questions about who we really are and the reality we find ourselves in. I find his words speak to my humanity, and remind me not to take things as they are for granted or to accept them if I think they can be better. The first words in the book are "Heaven knows we need poetry now more than ever. We need the awkward truth of poetry. We need its indirect insistence on the magic of listening... Poetry is closer to us than politics, and is as intrinsic to us as walking or eating." I recommend reading 'One Planet, One People – an address to students' because we are all learning no matter what age we are, and it is about the very core of being human and the possibilities before us. The things that Okri says in this poem are the things that we all know but few of us master.

Amisha Ghadiali

Recently I went to see Joan Miro's exhibition at the Tate Modern and I have to say it was probably one of the best exhibitions I've been to. Miro lived through a time of political instability in Spain (the Spanish Civil War) under the dictator Francisco Franco. All of this seeps through his work and career. He was greatly heavily influenced by the politics of that time. I really enjoyed his earlier paintings of the Catalan landscape but his Surrealist paintings are far more interesting. His paintings began to take on more abstract forms as objects and people are merely strokes of paint becoming part of his visual language. My favourite pieces were a series of large lithographs titled 'The Barcelona Series' in which he expresses his thoughts of tyranny. Images of large monsters' heads, mouths open revealing sharp teeth, one-eyed ogres - these were based on dictator Franco and Pére Ub. I admire Miro because when you look at his work it can be challenging but I think that's what art is all about. Art should provoke the viewers to think and make their own informed judgement.

Jo Cheung

I believe that the most important thing is an idea.
It's the beginning for all innovation and change.
It's a starting point in order to understand what has
to be done and which way you want to go.

Migle Vilkeliskyte

When my son, who is a wheelchair user, took part in his first sports day, all the children lined up, and the starting gun went off. The children set off, and everyone cheered as you would expect. But as the last child crossed the finishing line, Samuel was just half way down the track in his small powered chair. I waited to see what happened. The cheering subsided. But then a new noise began. People clapping and chanting Samuel's name as he finished the remainder of the race on his own, a huge look of determination on his face. We all tell our children "It's the taking part that counts, not the winning". Deep down, though, we all rather like it when our kids do win. But I can honestly say, that at that moment, it did become the taking part that counted, not the winning. Samuel's presence, in all his vulnerability, transformed the values of the sports day - for the better. If we allow the vulnerable, and those who are too often excluded, to enter into our world, and allow them to change it, then we can transform it for the better.

Jonathan Bartley

Education…. No matter what age you are, you can never stop learning and being inquisitive. Be it through formal education or not. We can never know everything, and while that is true, exploration of ourselves and the world we live in will never be complete. I am constantly inspired by books, films, music and the people around me, and I aim to be like this throughout my life. I am inspired by people on such a wide spectrum that includes activists like Wangari Maathai, who not only led a group of women from rural Kenya, but did so in a groundbreaking environmental movement; and authors like Haruki Murakami, whose books have fed my imagination and left me ever so slightly baffled for years!

Amy Haworth Johns

A life changing experience was my first Burning Man. Being out on the playa made me realize that I am really the only one that can be held responsible for my own happiness and influence. It made me aware of the fact that I already had all the tools I need to make a change: a vigorous mind, to think of the unimaginable, and a healthy body to act upon those thoughts.

Mariangela De Lorenzo

The abolition movement started in an underground cellar in London. The American revolutionaries gathered in pubs to debate their future. The Haitians organized in the forest, the Suffragettes gathered in secret behind their men's backs, Mandela built a movement from prison and today we can all talk to one another with the click of a button. The future is unbridled so I say let us claim it for our children and theirs.

Sean Carasso

Reading Joseph Campbell introduced me to an image taken from Indian folklore called 'the net of Indra'. The net of Indra is "a net of gems where, at every crossing of one thread over another, there is a gem reflecting all the other reflective gems. Everything arises in mutual relation to everything else". This image is a metaphor for the idea that as human beings, hard as we may try to delude ourselves, we are not, and never will be, islands unto ourselves. We are fundamentally interconnected with one another and the planet itself. When I really consider this, then injustice anywhere in the world compromises my own freedom, my own peace. An illusion of separateness is what leads to loneliness and apathy. A sense of being apart of a greater ecosystem liberates us from the cage of our egos and empowers us with responsibility.

Meredith Hines

I read voraciously, but the book of relationships is the richest and most inexhaustible. The most important thought is taking a moment to listen, really listen, to what the person facing you is saying or not quite saying. See your own face through their eyes. Listen to their hopes and fears and dreams, and listen for the echoes chiming in your own heart. It's not simple or easy, this. It can lead to all kinds of arguments and embarrassments. But it's the beginning of everything that is good and human.

Paul Hilder

ACTS

YOUR ACT IS SOMETHING
THAT WE CAN ALL START
DOING TODAY TO HELP
CREATE THE FUTURE
THAT YOU CHOOSE

I love Baroness Cox's motto: "I cannot do everything, but I must not do nothing". I like the idea of finding something you're passionate about and just doing something.

Anila Babla

Keep a gratitude journal, to note at least 5 things at the end of each day that you were grateful for.

Kiran Patel

Nowadays it's so easy to get caught up in the 'busyness' that's almost expected of you and to lose sight of the fact that your life is actually your own. The following is an Act that helps me to stop and reconfigure my priorities. Spend a quiet half hour visualising your ideal typical day and try and record it in some way (writing, drawing etc.). Consider where you are, who's around you and what activities you undertake through the course of the day. What does your environment look like? How do you feel? Be as descriptive as possible, consider all your senses, and don't hold back. Revisit this exercise as regularly as necessary to remind yourself to act in alignment with your vision.

Lulu Kitololo

Flowers. Look at them. Pick them. Paint them. Photograph them. Smell them. Grow them. Flowers.

Palvi Raikar

Winston Smith from George Orwell's 1984 or Guy Montag from Ray Bradbury's Fahrenheit 941: both protagonists, Smith and Montag, find themselves working under governments whose main objective is suppressing human thought and eliminating human individuality. Yet both defy the odds and risk their lives, simply to be able to retain their ability to think individual and distinctive thoughts. Hopefully we will end up having some Winstons and Montags of our own or else we might end up like this.

I love discovering and reading the stories of individuals who have gone against the flow and tried to defy stereotypical standards. JR's current project, Inside Out, is using art and photography to turn the world literally inside out. To see individuals that we encounter everyday in a new light. And what's amazing is that anyone can do it.

Moreover I think to be able to act you need a spark of inspiration. I get mine from simple observation, from videos on the net, from people, from my surroundings, from friends, from family, from strangers, from art, from reading, from everything really. If you want to be inspired to change then you can be.

Dina Yunis

I think an Act we can all do to help create the future is to get in touch with our inner selves, to understand that it starts with the soul, the spirit, the higher self, the inner self - whatever you want to call it. We need to get in touch with that inside voice of ours - the good voice I suppose - as opposed to all the noise. I think that's part of the journey really and the easiest way to do that is through meditation, whatever your religious practices or your beliefs, or your 'no beliefs'! I believe that meditation, having stillness, going inside, whether it's through yoga or however it may be in these busy lives we all lead, is crucial.

Lynne Franks

Set aside 5 minutes a day to take a little of the news in and give it some consideration. I tend to swim in news but am conscious that most people don't want to do that; but people do need to be engaged at some level because the essential problem with democracy is, if you don't use it, you do tend to lose it. Maybe you are rightly angry with politicians over an issue like expenses - good, you should be, but don't just get angry: get even, and get involved.

Darrell Goodliffe

Charles Clarke had an ambition to put philosophy on the school curriculum. I hate the elitist connotations the word philosophy has, but I was always struck by how little I was led towards independent thought at school. I would teach it from a very young age. Perhaps then I could say 'epistemic duty' and people wouldn't look at me like I was a loser.

Patrick Hussey

Start with changing the way we spend - or waste - our time. Trying something new - whether it's visiting a soup kitchen for the homeless for an hour, hearing from a politician we wouldn't usually listen to, starting a for-profit company that aims to pay its fair share of taxes, or even offering to spend an afternoon visiting the elderly neighbours who live alone - is a great start.

Jag Singh

There is a spectrum of various acts that we can all do. First, ensure you put your own litter in a bin or take it home with you. Second, how about picking up at least one piece of someone else's litter a day. Third, how about doing a litter pick where you live. Next, why not organise a litter pick where you live and, finally, how about forming a group of your fellow-residents to keep your area tidy and to encourage others to do so?

George Monck

Make a list of what it is you think you can offer to the world and tick one thing off in the next week.

Libby James

I believe we change the world by changing ourselves. We need to get right with ourselves and heal. Whether it's therapy, going into recovery, learning meditation, practicing yoga, or keeping a journal, cultivate a practice that draws you inward, keeps you honest, and brings you some clarity. When enough individuals transform their interior landscape from a war zone to a place of peace, the outside world will follow suit.

Meredith Hines

Let go of fear.

Zara Martin

Take a minute.
Stand on the edge of a cliff
and catch the gaze of the horizon.
Take a breath and listen.
Come back and tell me what you discovered.

Annegret Affolderbach

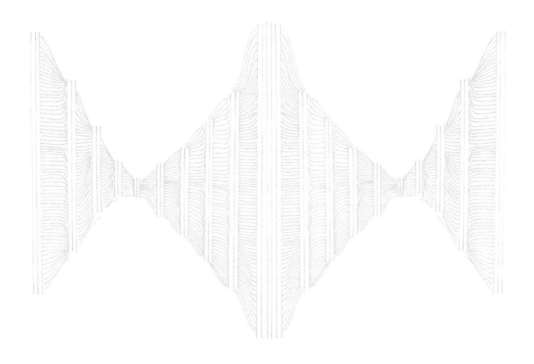

Stand up for what you believe in. It may sound a cliché, but it is needed now more than ever. Over the last three decades, as employment and livelihoods have become increasingly "flexible" and ever more precarious, we have been made to believe that there's little space for demanding many of our rights. This is only a perception. We have to demand better from those in power.

Sarah Ditty

There's an Act for a better future lying hidden in every moment, but here's one simple one that I at least have found can teach patience, consequence and reward. Plant a seed with someone you care about. Tend it, water it and feed it. Watch it grow, day after day, into something tasty or beautiful or both. Share the joy and plant again.

Paul Hilder

Sit down and make a list of the things you have to offer. It really is amazing when you realise what you already have - not just physical items, but talent. Then join your Local Exchange Trading Scheme (LETS) or *justfortheloveofit.org* where you can share what you already have in exchange for what you need. It is amazing to give and receive in this way.

Gloria Charles

Take time to understand the realities of social and environmental issues. Learn to think critically. Take action when needed. Write to your local council about milk deliveries.

Gareth Barnes

Be interested, slow down at least once a week and discover something new. Get active, and learn the happiness in keeping fit; to discover, by listening, that everyone has a story worth telling; to unlock the pleasure in culture, education, history or the arts... to do all these things, or something completely different, but just to be interested.

Emily Wilkie

Add data feed to *pachube.com*. Look up things you've bought on *sourcemap.com* and try to help map the supply chain. Publicly (via social media perhaps) question advertising that could be greenwash. If it isn't greenwash the company will soon reply with a verified report or certification. Monitor your energy usage. Get interested in data and the visualisation of it; this will be key to changing behaviour.

Jessi Baker

Choose to create one thing a day – and be aware that you are choosing to do so. This could be singing a song to a child, writing a postcard to a friend, taking a picture, knitting a few stitches, cooking a meal.
Or simply creating a moment of stillness and being mindful of your breathing. This year I have been taking one photograph a day, and I have found that I have become more aware of and connected to the world around me through taking the time to see.

Olivia Sprinkel

Stay in the moment and just get stuff done. Straight through. Stay positive. Be honest to yourself. Love your lover, your family and your friends.

Joao Machado

"Personal Change = Social Change," I think an Act we should all be doing is introspection, self-reflection and deepening our knowledge of self. Whether that's through writing in a journal, taking five minutes of quiet time a day, talking to a coach or therapist, finding a book that helps us dive deeper into ourselves--whatever process works for you, as long as you're taking time to pause and thoughtfully reflect on who you are, who you've been and who you want to be. We walk around with a lot of wounds that go unhealed, ultimately being projected onto others. We also walk around distracted by all the flashing billboards telling us what we should want for our lives, how we should look, act and think. Our unique selves and special gifts, that we were given to share with the world, get lost and buried under past shame, or in the hustle to be like somebody else. The more we acknowledge the beauty in owning our whole selves, for better and for worse, the more empowered we will be to make change. As Biggie Smalls said, "We can't change the world, unless we change ourselves."

Ariana Proehl

Be kind to yourself, be kind to others. Smile at strangers. Make kind gestures to people you've never met before: let someone with fewer items go ahead of you in the queue at the supermarket, step aside for the person who clearly looks like they're rushing. Look at the world through someone else's eyes. If someone has made you think or has made your day better or has created something that has moved you, tell them.

Kellee Rich

Choose to cycle as much as possible. To sow seeds and cultivate diverse flowers. Eat as diverse a diet as you possibly can. Try wild foods. Learn about your surroundings. Observe. Be still. Open your eyes. Be kind and see the other person as you, to grow humanity and empathy. Share stories and dreams with as many as possible. Create cognitive resonance for the new world we aspire to live in and co-create together. Talk about it! Everywhere!

Lucy Gilliam

You don't need to be a hero and get murdered to change the world. Sometimes even a simple and small act can positively affect the order of things. Refuse to be cynical, to passively accept the world as it is.

Maria Teresa Sette

My personal mission at the moment is to encourage 'Microadventures' as a way of getting people outdoors, learning to love wildness, challenging themselves, and refocusing on what is really important to them.

Alistair Humphreys

Respect should always be given, deserved or not, and Love should be shown... simply hug everyone you meet and greet.

Jeff Garner

Make an inspiration board, find all the things that excite you and spark your energy, stick a picture of them on a special board; look at it daily and feel the energy of inspiration.

Lucy White

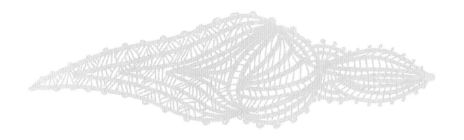

Make better decisions about where you spend your
mental time and energy. It's easy in a world that is filled
with so many stimuli to be distracted, and to always feel
as if we're wanting something or missing something
in our lives. When we've been programmed to want
more, and to compare ourselves to others constantly,
it's easy to be dissatisfied. I would suggest taking
a few moments out of every day to just be quiet ...
to just reflect or to not do anything at all.
We need to get comfortable with silence.

Philip McKenzie

Actively be a part of where you live.
Introduce yourself to your neighbours, support your local shopkeepers, smile at people on the way to the tube, invite your friends over, find out what's going on and get involved... I've had great BBQs with neighbours and been there to help when they were locked out, and have shopped at the same greengrocer for 7 years (he even let me leave with everything when I forgot my wallet one time).
About a year ago I turned up to help an urban farming hub in Hackney, and now run events and activities there. I've made a ton of new friends, and together we've created a welcoming urban green space.
A place feels more like home when you know people's names. Find volunteering opportunities near you through do-it.

Laura Billings

I agree with Dave Eggers when he called upon the TED community and the world to get involved with a local school. But make it broader, and ask people to connect with young people - especially, but not exclusively, the disadvantaged and the marginalised - and to talk to them, to ask them questions about how they envision their future, what their aspirations are, and to help them realise their ambitions. This doesn't have to be confined to schools: it could be done through a mentorship scheme or through a work placement programme, or through any other route available to them. Also listen to other people carefully, rather than just picking out the bits you want to hear. That includes listening tothe people who disagree with you. Listen to what they say, and try to understand why they are saying it. Societies favour some over others: where do you fit in? Where does the person talking fit in? What can you do collectively to make your society fairer? My Act will really count when others are acting too.

Eugenie Teasley

Be more considerate, be it through giving, sharing, or just taking the time to listen more. Even small gestures are valued, be it hand-making the presents you give your friends and family to show them just how important they are, or seeking out ways in which you could help other people directly.

Kirstie Battson

Turn off the TV, step away from your laptop and take time to look, listen, feel, smell and enjoy the world around you. Unless we connect with our communities and the world we share we won't value and understand them. We won't take the time to realise how important they are. We will lose them. Once we empathise with the world, then we can understand what we all need to do to create a future we all want to share. This takes time: to listen and learn, to test and to act, to begin the process of creating that world. The Acts are to be open, to listen (and not judge), to engage, to learn, reflect and share.

Simon Goldsmith

If you spot someone doing something well, be sure to give him or her a compliment! It can be easy to find faults and we often only speak up when we have something to complain about, so I think it would be a great idea if we could be more open about the good stuff too.

Rhea Babla

Here's a common theme I would like to see change. You go to a shop and greet the person working there. They won't even acknowledge you or look you in the eye. You apply for a job; you don't even get a letter of rejection. You don't want your country to go to war, so you march and protest - but it falls on deaf ears. At what point do you become human again, and not just another face in a crowd?

I would like people to be better to each other. It's a small start towards having some compassion, and making the future a better one. I think the bigger implications are everywhere - from providing a great education to a productive debate in parliament. Contempt and cynicism can be too easy and attractive a viewpoint, when the harder, more positive thing is to smile and encourage people who feel they don't have a voice. Or that they don't have a future, because it's all in someone else's hands.

There are issues relating to everything - poverty, lack of education, mental health and job satisfaction - when being listened to, and even empowered to better the system, could be to the benefit of all. But starting small, one day and one smile at a time, seems more realistic. Make friends. Make people laugh. Life's far too short.

Mike Harman

Thinking, or being conscious of our attitudes, can build a better future. When I personally made self-awareness an exercise, I was able to develop a much better understanding of how easy it is to change. The book 'Awakening the Buddha Within' by Lama Surya Das is a good tool. Learn how to make clever choices, the ones that are motivated by a great outcome; if you can, make choices thinking that we are part of one society that you can choose to make your community.

Alicia Bastos

Talk to people. I walk almost everywhere and sometimes just stopping to talk to an elderly person can make their whole week seem brighter. Or go to an event and find some interesting people to speak to, hear what they have to say and let them inspire you. Talk to someone successful and make his or her position your goal. If they did it, who says you can't do the same thing? Or something bigger and greater? Have faith and confidence in yourself!

Abrar Agil

Not everyone does – recycle as if second nature.

Philip Levine

Meditate.

Maria Papadimitriou

Talk to somebody you normally wouldn't talk to and listen to their story. I was on set a few months ago (and I'd say I'm pretty open minded) and we had a guy working with us who had tons and tons of tattoos, was an ex-gang member and had just come out of prison 5-6 months previously.
He looked like the kind of guy you probably wouldn't want to meet down a dark alley! I found myself very aware of the fact he looked quite menacing so I made a point of going up and talking to him and he sat and told me about his life story and it was the saddest thing.

This man was now trying to change his life and turn it around to create a better life for his children. He was working as a runner on this particular production I was working on and I thought "Wow, this is somebody who probably comes up against this all the time; and it would be hard for someone like that to change their life - because of the way we see people in society and the way we are so reluctant to give people a second chance."

I think that is definitely one of the things I would say - go and talk to somebody you wouldn't normally talk to, someone who actually makes you feel a bit uncomfortable.

June Sarpong

Find warmth in yourself to succeed, live your dreams and share positive ideas. Forget all negativity and live your life according to you.

Sara Abdel-Hamid

Be part of a community. Communities are powerful groups that can create change but also protect things.

Chris Arnold

Do everything you always do, but be just that little bit more curious. And every time you feel an itch to condemn something, remind yourself that itch is probably there for a good reason. Follow that reason.

Oliver Moody

Instead of judging someone on what they believe or where they're from, find out more about them, get to know them and open your mind to new things. Not everybody is the same, and there is a lot more to an individual than meets the eye.

Laura Anderson

Politicians are a vested interest group, only in politics to get re-elected: we should let them know by letter and email what our views are and tell them that if they don't represent our views in parliament we won't vote for them next time. We need to get our elected representatives to represent the majority view of their constituency on every issue, no more toeing the party line and being forced to vote with the government. We can do this by having national and constituency referenda, and a civil service to implement them and administer the country according to the results. If we had had this, we wouldn't have had an illegal war in Iraq, with thousands of innocent lives lost. We wouldn't be cutting much-needed A&Es. We wouldn't be having to cut child benefit so we can pay bankers' bonuses. It's our country and we as citizens should decide how it's run; it's our money, we should decide how it is spent. We can use our vote to get the country we want.

Katharine Hamnett

We cannot learn from natural ecosystems if the species they comprise become extinct. Act now to protect biodiversity by not only applying the three R's – reduce, reuse, recycle, but by sourcing every product and service you need responsibly. By taking these simple steps you will take ownership of your role in protecting Earth's biodiversity.

Melissa Sterry

Spend less time with computers, TVs, smartphones ... Go outside and breath more often, hug more people, spend more time with family.

Joana Casaca Lemos

We can all just try to be a better person, to be more considerate of the people around us and more aware of the consequences of our choices on the environment. It's a lesson we can pass on to our children and all around us.
Be the role model.

Rachel Saw

I think we need to comprehend that we are moving into a post-geographical world... time and distance don't have to be barriers to participation... creed, religion etc are obsolete. The internet connects our MINDS directly and we can form new communities based on shared passions... collaboration and cooperation expanding at exponential rates ... I think we need to cultivate and curate our social networks well just so that we don't get overwhelmed by the "vertigo of freedom".

Jason Silva

Have an opinion! It's not just acceptable to like Wayne McGregor and Glee simultaneously; it's to be celebrated! There absolutely is objectively excellent 'popular' work, and there is absolutely dreadful 'high art' work. The key is in being able to separate what you've been told is great and what you believe to be great.

Peter Gregson

Ask questions! We now have so many tools to look for information that we should be a bit more curious about the world around us.

Aurélie Dumont

Find other like minds and create.
Don't sit around waiting for that record contract/book deal/audition etc but take what you do directly to an audience. If all the out-of-work artists got together and did it themselves, they would rival all the massive record companies/studios etc. Artists should collaborate rather than compete. If you enjoy art (in all/any of its forms) you can be more selective in your choices and not just pick mainstream options. You can give people a voice and be encouraged to have yours heard.

Lucie Barât

Do something that challenges you, you'll be surprised at what you can do. Do something where you can be creative, and you'll want to learn even more. Do something crafty, and you can interpret that as you wish!

Noel Hatch

Smile at strangers – it's something small but impactful. Try it! 9 times out of 10 that you smile at someone they will smile too.
Then add a good morning to it and even better! As Gandhi says 'be the change you wish to see' – if something bothers you, go and work in that field, go and campaign, go and help out; do your part. We have one life and it should be one that positively affects others we encounter.

Jacqueline Shaw

"Seize the day": it's a famous saying that I interpret myself as to do something now, rather than tomorrow, if you can.

Alex Smith

I believe in making. Make as much as you can - it means so much more. The craft company that I co-founded uses recycled objects, making them into new, quirky products. Make your Christmas presents this year - it means a lot more to people when you tell them you made it yourself! Upcycle your old clothes and make bags, cushions, table runners, chair covers, new clothing. Think of the money you'll save, as well as your contribution to the future you are creating!

Vicky Fallon

Borrowing from Ghandi: Be the generosity you wish to see in the world. In the widest sense of the word too, it's so much more than giving money. For example, forgiveness is generosity of thought.

Pete Yeo

Question the services we all use when we are online and ask yourself whether they are inherently open or inherently closed. For example, Apple Computer is inherently closed and, although they make a lot of money and some really fabulous products, their code is as secret as the recipe for Coca Cola. Compare Apple now with Linux computer systems that are Open Source and build on each succeeding version by allowing anyone to identify bugs and improve it. So next time you are prompted to check the "agree" button on a "terms of service" for an app or a website you are subscribing to, go back and actually read it and you will start to realize there is a clear line in the sand between OPEN and CLOSED.

Andrew Rasiej

The best Act you can do is to simply act. 99% of us say we'll do things and don't. Just do one thing you said you'd do, do it well, and if all of us did that, what a difference it'd make.

Chris Arnold

105

If you encounter a challenge, try to look for a root cause by asking the question 'Why does that happen?' over and over again. When you get to a dead end, that's probably the thing that needs to change. Also, try to be more aware of what you're thinking / feeling while you're actually feeling it. We're good at being aware of our physical movement, like waving our arms (it's called proprioception) but it's not so easy with attitudes or emotions. There's not even a word for it!

Matt Chocqueel-Mangan

Buy less crap – and there's a lot of it out there. Don't follow fads: there's no need to have the latest gadget/clothing/car/iPhone/stereo/console/shoes…

Christian Smith

Contact your MP and make them aware of your position. Ask them to raise this issue in Parliament and seek to change this. Don't let people make you believe you can't do something just because it doesn't fit in with their agenda.

Umair Baig

Ask yourself the question, what makes me feel vulnerable? Explore that, and try to understand what feels scary about it and then take a step to feel vulnerable and notice what you feel, what you experience. Share with others what it felt like, what you discovered and see if you can start a mini-movement of vulnerability being seen as something that gives strength, rather than a sign of weakness.

Cassie Robinson

Take responsibility and self-educate yourself as to how products are made, where they are made and use social media to start conversations with big chains as to their manufacturing processes. There really is no excuse, with the Internet, for not finding things out for yourself: the best education is now available online. Also, try to consume less and be really careful about where your products come from. Try to buy locally, from traceable suppliers, and don't be afraid to ask questions about where your food, clothes and products come from. With a more open conversation between consumers and suppliers, and a willingness to learn from each other, changes are more easily made.

Rachel Holland

Speak up. Be educated in what is said and stand by it. An Act is to never shy away from taking a position, controversial as it may be. As Voltaire said, "I disagree with what you say but I will fight to the death your right to say it".

Miguel Fernandes Ceia

Purchase products with biodegradable wrapping, or none at all; remove the demand to stop the supply.

Alison Day

Encourage companies that outsource, or get their basic resources from a developing country, to agitate for and demand and create the infrastructures in the developing world that they do have here in the United Kingdom. So if you're in the petro-carbon and gas industry, if you're in manufacturing, if you're in agriculture, the standards you have to work with in this country or any G34 country are the standards you should operate in the sourcing country. If you work to those exact standards, I think that by osmosis you positively affect the indigenous population. If someone goes into a factory in Africa or Asia, they then also go into the local community, and by definition their experiences then begin to touch the people in the local populations.

We have had postcolonial exploitation of developing nations, such as that demonstrated by massive petro-chemical companies, who don't care about spoiling the environment when drilling for the oil. The people can't fish there anymore, can't farm there anymore, they can't utilise their own basic resources. We can drive our cars and have lights on all day, but they can't put fish on the table and that's wrong. You have got to put the pipes so deep that they don't percolate to the top; you have got to make sure people don't damage the pipes and spoil the land; you have got to demand that governments do the same, so that a leader isn't going to nick millions of dollars of oil, but instead put it back into the community where it comes from.

People who work in developing countries need to work within the same standards of practice as they do in the developed world. If everyone did that then the world would be a better place to live. If the leaders of governments had legislation on the way they operate overseas - I am not talking about lip service, but actual legislation in developing countries, as we have in this country - the world would be a better place. We all know the world is corrupt, there's corruption in developing countries, there's corruption in this country. In developed worlds, we've got banking problems; we've got fraud and dishonesty such as MPs expense fiddling. We know that people are corrupt all over the world but there is a difference between the developed and the developing world: even with the corrupt practices in the developed world, we are still assured of our infrastructure being maintained. In the developing world, they have the same type of corrupt practices but they don't have the infrastructure, so it's incumbent upon those of us who have, and see the light, to shed the light in those other areas.

Kriss Akabusi

The biggest problem facing the world is not hunger, disease, water, lack of education, war, corruption... it is apathy: the fact that we can see problems around us, but do nothing. So pledge to give up apathy, to do something, to do one thing to help make a better world.

Michael Norton

An Act is just that - to simply get on and do it. Whatever it is, however small, stop putting it off. I struggle with this a lot, especially when I know that what I have to do is important, such as getting in touch with someone who I know could have a brilliantly positive impact on my campaign work. The spectre of failure can become paralysing. 'What if they say no, what then?' But you have to get over yourself. The best thing I've read to inspire you to get on and do it is right here.

Hanna Thomas

Become more involved with politics and understand that it is not simply the 'grey and old' that should be making decisions which impose upon everyone. We all have a part to play and so should take an active approach towards it. The basic principle of being an active citizen is, of course, voting. People should at least start with that as it has the potential to make a huge difference.

Lina Jovaisaite

Implement your ideas! Start from yourself, believe in yourself and ideas will transform into everyday acts.

Migle Vilkeliskyte

Use social media in a constructive way. I know we all like to log into Facebook and see where our friends are spending their summers, or who went to which party; but really, that's a pretty lame use when you realize that the same thing that you're already logging into every day has the potential to liberate countries, galvanize youth movements, or turn mind-blowing scientific discoveries into water-cooler discourse. Be a curator for change; you may start a domino effect.

Max Lugavere

Well... in a perfect world, people that care would do things about the environment around them, and the simplest way of doing that is to become an elective member of your local council. Now... if you look at some of the more progressive countries in Europe, the Scandinavian countries especially, you'll find elected councillors in their 20s and 30s who are representing that generation. If you go to a lot of towns in the UK you'll find the average age of a lot of the council that are supposedly representing the whole of their community, and making decisions on our behalf, can be around late 60s and 70s. Now there's nothing wrong with that - I'm not saying there's anything wrong with old people - but you cannot expect all 60 odd-year-olds and 70 year-olds to totally understand what a 15 year old or a 20 year old wants out of the future... so we can only make that difference; you know... I'm 51 and I would still be considered a young council member and I'm not young.

Wayne Hemingway

If you're someone that makes more than $2 a day, understand how incredibly fortunate you are and, acknowledging that, do your part to try and make things a little fairer for those less fortunate.

Graham Hill

Follow a simple routine that involves: connection, competence, confidence. I need to connect or connect people with one another; I learn, teach or coach someone into harnessing their skills, and developing their ventures. Finally, I need to give myself confidence that the whole vision is a step nearer everyday, and/or create a platform for an individual, their team, or a whole group to gain confidence and create more impact. So if a woman impresses you for the changes she brings about around her (even small), make sure people know about her, tell her story to the local press, and in turn to tell your friends to listen to her, and tell others about her...

Servane Mouazan

Inform yourself with current affairs and different ways of looking at the world. Talk to people. Try and curb your time with social media and just get on and DO IT.

Petronella Tyson

Don't look down on people because they are different, accept them. Don't hate people for having a different religious viewpoint to you, respect them.

Rubi Anwar

Think about what you wear. Clothes are an important part of our daily lives, and the fashion industry employs one sixth of the world's population. We have the opportunity to affect millions of people's lives and to protect our environment by how we shop and what we wear. Fashion production is riddled with environmental and social problems from toxic chemical dumping to human rights abuses. We all need to be more conscious about what we let into our wardrobes, what we do with things that we don't want anymore and how we stand up to companies that are putting money before our planet and the people involved in making our clothes. How can we enjoy expressing ourselves through fashion, or the comfort and warmth of clothes, if what we are wearing has caused pain and destruction on its way to us?

Amisha Ghadiali

Help create a co-op in your community and purchase goods that are ethically produced.

Christian Flores Carignan

Meditate, pray, or engage in some form of silent, calm emptiness for at least five minutes a day. Over time, you'll find that the thoughts and feelings that have arisen in those periods of silence are some of the most meaningful, transformative, and vivid human experiences. A society of people who are in touch with themselves is a more harmonious and constructive society.

Ted Gonder

Consumers have so much power. It's so easy to forget that people have been involved in the making of every item you ever purchase. It's easier than ever to find out where the product has come from and if there are any ethical credentials to it. There are also so many options now; you don't have to compromise on style or quality to purchase something with a positive story behind it.

Joanna Maiden

Live with a conscience. It we are all aware of - or at least make an effort to learn about - the consequences of our actions, the world will be a much nicer place. We won't always know the knock-on effects, so we can't chastise ourselves for that, but we can live with grace, sensibility and respect.

Ellie Good

I believe in a collective responsibility to actively protect the vulnerable, using whatever we have at our disposal. We all have skills and talents that we develop during the pursuit of our own happiness. I believe we must ACT – we have a responsibility to use our business acuity and training, not only to accrue material possessions and privileges for ourselves, but also to object to and propose solutions to injustice. For my part, I attempt to combine my skills with voluntary work for the Medical Foundation for Victims of Torture, Holloway Women's Prison, the Circle and Hogar Villegas orphanage in Bolivia.

A good campaign to get involved in is the Raising Her Voice campaign in Eastern Africa. RHV aims to influence public policy, decision-making, and expenditure to reflect the interests of women from poor countries, and one of their focuses is quickening the domestication of the Maputo Protocol on the rights of women in places like Uganda; a group of lawyers, including me, travelled there this summer to speak with government departments and see whether we could assist. There are frustrating dead ends in the constitutional protection of the rights of women, in part because the people who would benefit from the Protocol are powerless. When people cannot vote freely, or when their votes mean nothing, how crucial it is that we, who can, ACT positively to enact change.

Karis McLarty

It's our responsibility to redesign our own world. Don't look away. Do speak up. It's also your own future, your own environment. Come up with alternatives to make steps forward. Take away 'tension points'.

Arjan Hoffman

An old friend once said to me that these days the most radical thing we can do is make our own fun. If we can rely on ourselves and each other to make life joyful, everything else feels a little more manageable.

Andy Gibson

I'm intrigued by how many people aren't really doing what they want to do. I feel like so many people I meet say 'I'm doing this now, but really I'd like to...be a film maker...travel the world...be an actor...change the world.' So my Act, for me, and for everyone who's ever said something like that, is to just do it. Do anything. Do something. Something is always better than nothing. Follow your passion. Take risks. Take big steps or take baby steps; just take steps. You might stumble. But you might just achieve your dreams.

Alexis Wieroniey

Dance, sing (no matter how badly), read, watch, observe, travel, participate, love, live, learn, listen, laugh, absorb, grow, cook, create, walk, explore, help, form friendships, believe, SMILE.

Amy Haworth Jones

Take the 24 hour challenge. For 24 hours say nothing negative and think nothing negative. Each time you do, start the 24 hours again. When you can do 24 hours, do a week. When you can do a week, do a month. Each time you say or think anything negative, start again. When you can do a month, Keep Going. The benefits are powerful. Negative is toxic. It poisons your ability to inspire people and to have people trust you. It lowers your energy level and depletes your enthusiasm. Positive talk to yourself and others is life enhancing to yourself and others.

Tim Drake

The Act that has in my opinion the power to create a future (where the present would be sufficient) is the awareness of Love. Love, to me, is the unknown we know by heart. An unknown, a mystery that we can all understand when we stop trying to comprehend it and simply follow our intuition.

Bruno Pieters

An Act is the motion/ movement/ gesture you offer to the cause that you have chosen to change. It gives the 'think' a form and expression. I think we are now, more than ever, in a time when mindful action is needed. If we can find a point at which we connect with others, or act in a way in which we can access the intersections with other people and nature, we can create a more equitable way of living.

Lauren Craig

Spend time with nature, natural habitats, surrounded by wildlife. It's a great way to realise the greater picture that we belong to. It is very easy to become involved in a digital existence but the reality is that we are on a planet made of earth, water, fire, wind and space.

Tia Kansara

If we all spoke up when we felt something wasn't right, the world would be a much better place. When we feel something is wrong, we should ask questions. "All that is required for evil to prevail is for good [people] to do nothing," said Edmund Burke - Irish statesperson, author, orator, political theorist and philosopher in the 18th century. A racist comment? A sexist act? Unjust treatment? Speak up. Ask a question. Let's put ourselves forward. Let's recognise that fear is only a bad thing when it stops us from doing something. Feel the fear and, at the same time, do what we think is right.

Laura Nelson

VOTES

YOUR VOTE IS A PLEDGE
OF ALLEGIANCE TO
SOMETHING THAT YOU
BELIEVE IS CREATING
THE FUTURE YOU CHOOSE.

....

My Vote is to do my bit to challenge the status quo gracefully and fearlessly.
My Vote is to inspire balance, harmony and the beauty of simplicity by employing my talents as a designer and writer.
My Vote is to speak my truths without dressing them up.
My Vote is to inspire fairness and kindness by making the processes in my work sustainable from the word go; to be fair and kind to people and our planet.
My Vote is to put a transparent price tag on the products I create. Making the processes and the stories behind my products transparent and accessible, both to consumers and producers, will help them unite in discovery and knowledge. This notion of transparent trade will provide true and honest choices for each person engaged with the product. It provides a direct lifeline between consumers and producers, putting value back into each skill deployed and each purchase made.

Annegret Affolderbach

....

A Vote 'X' is when you cross your heart: holding, supporting, being. I connect voting more to a political stance. Although we can vote through where we 'click' or where we buy, or who we choose as friends,
I think voting is about standing up and being counted for your values. I vote for a future that doesn't depend on the exploitation of farming countries. I vote for hyper-local, community-based, sustainable living systems simultaneously with a vote for ethical global supply chains, for gender equality and for human, working and planetary rights.

Lauren Craig

....

Qualities that make us human are being, and
understanding that we are, greater when we work
together than when we are alone. Examples of this
are online movements such as Avaaz and Change for
global issues and 38 Degrees for those in the UK.
Not only do these sites alert us to what is going on
in the world, but allow us to participate in a global
democracy without borders or parties. Through their
campaigns we can create a better world, one issue
at a time.
www.avaaz.org
www.change.org
www.38degrees.org.uk

....

Petronella Tyson

As consumers we can be very powerful in driving change. An example is the project we started 6 years ago, the fair trade brand of trainers Veja. Working directly with cooperatives of small farmers across Brazil, we use organic cotton, wild rubber from the Amazon and naturally-tanned leather to create the Veja trainers and accessories. From the fields of raw materials in Brazil to the doors of the fashion stores in Europe, where the sneakers and accessories are available, we try to respect very high social and environmental standards. This means a thorough involvement in agro-ecology farming initiatives in North Brazil, in the fight against deforestation in the Amazon, in workers' rights and dignity protection, and also in social rehabilitation back in Europe.
www.veja.fr

Aurélie Dumont

I like the 10:10 initiative, which appeals to both consumers and companies and works with easy, reachable goals.
www.1010global.org

Arjan Hoffman

By donating what you no longer need to the Red Cross, you also help this humanitarian organization in aiding people in distress worldwide.
www.ifrc.org

Alison Day

My Vote right now is to appreciate our universal interconnectedness and support the millions of people suffering in the East African region as a result of the food crisis in the Horn of Africa. One way to support the starving in Kenya is through the Red Cross appeal.
www.kenyaredcross.org

Lulu Kitololo

Big charities do have a role, they have political clout, they have people at the top who are meeting with heads of state, heads of industry. But small charities like mine, The Akabusi Charitable Trust, have a role as well, because we are meeting on the ground with the people who really matter; we are seeing it with our eyes, we're observing the development of our programs, and ensuring that the woman herself gets the capacity built in to sustain her business, well after we're gone; whereas, a big charity often builds a big infrastructure, drops lots of money off, but then goes off somewhere else and doesn't know what happens with that.

We work in the real communities in Nigeria. We're very much in our infancy. We work with women: we have a programme called Women2Women where a woman in this country gives £100 to support the businesses of women in Nigerian communities. That £100 helps a woman invest in her children, invest in other children in the area, and build an infrastructure. I don't have the layers of political infrastructure, I just go straight into the interior, straight into the area my mother and father came from, Imo State, and I can actually help a real person I see. The money goes straight there, not on a mass of bureaucracy.
www.akabusitrust.org

Kriss Akabusi

Vote for tariffs against despots.
A sliding scale of import tariffs
against measures of human
rights and pension rights in each
country. I don't know of any group
or petition to support this idea,
so I hope this page inspires
someone else to set the system up.

John Robertson

Build Africa is the NGO I work for. I love what I do and I love to get up every morning. The organisation works to empower individuals to make a better life for themselves. Not to give a hand out, but a hand up. It is continually striving to do more and do it better, and to never settle for anything less. They have my Vote and it is a privilege to be a part of it.
www.build-africa.org

Libby James

It's so easy to get frustrated with the world, our lives and everyday problems that we forget that there are those who don't even have access to basic human rights, such as clean water. My Vote goes to Fresh2o - an incredible organisation that is helping raise awareness, and funds, for the global provision of clean water and sanitation. I'm extremely proud and honoured to be a part of their campaign.
www.fresh2o.org

Zara Martin

You can vote through what you wear every day. Join my campaign to make our wardrobes sustainable. I put together a poster and wardrobe shopping checklist called '12 Rules to Dress By.' This is designed to help us shop and dress in a way that considers the affects to people and the planet. Rules are made to be broken, but by following these you can make a difference.
www.elegancerebellion.com/rulestodressby

Amisha Ghadiali

One organisation I have been impressed by recently is 'Peace One Day' - you can vote for peace by supporting their call for a Global Truce on 21 September 2012. Peace is non-violence in all its forms – from peace at home, to peace in our countries. And one day of peace does make a difference – for example 4.5 million children have been vaccinated against polio in Afghanistan on the Peace Days in the last four years.
www.peaceoneday.org

Olivia Sprinkel

Every thought, act and feeling that we choose contains a Vote for the future we want. If I choose to respond with anger and separation, and choose not to change or examine that response, I'm voting for anger and separation for my future and campaigning on its behalf. If I choose to be playful and loving, to laugh and forgive, that's my Vote for the future I choose.

Lucy White

Of the many organisations standing on the frontline of environmental conservation, my Vote lays with Greenpeace and WWF, who unite world-class expertise, creativity and networks to help build a more sustainable future. Both are second-to-none at utilizing people power to tackle the issues that really count.
www.greenpeace.org
www.wwf.org.uk

Melissa Sterry

I really like the work of 'Sustain'. Campaigning for a better food system. Happy foods, supporting happy diverse environments and farming practices, are key to a happy healthy society.
www.sustainweb.org

Lucy Gilliam

Research volunteer databases like Vinspired and Do-It Volunteering. That way you can get work experience, and help out your community (AND the world, whilst you're at it!)
www.vinspired.com
www.do-it.org.uk

Tizane Navea-Rogers

My project 'What One Change' asks which one change would have the biggest positive impact on society? Anyone can share their one change, and I hope it will help to identify vital root causes of social change.

www.whatonechange.co.uk

Matt Chocqueel-Mangan

There are so many wonderful causes out there and I don't really think that one is any more important than another in some ways, and certainly there are some very effective ones. But if you feel in your heart that you care more about the environment, or animals or bees, or stopping women being raped everyday in the Congo - I certainly feel strongly about sexual violence anywhere in the world - then that's the path we have to follow. I wouldn't just pick out one or the other.

However, I do think it's important to get in touch with our heart and see what resonates, and then take action. Most of all I think it's about being part of a community - I think community is the future. Whether it's a global or local community, as we all connect with each other, we can do far more at grassroots level that we can do through nation states and politics. It's about connecting with your community and taking responsibility; that I, together with my sister, my brother, my neighbour, my mother, my daughter, my friend, can make a difference by collaboration, by connection.

Lynne Franks

My personal campaign is to buy only fairly traded, organic and English based products - I think if everybody would do the same we would suddenly see supermarket shelves beaming with seasonal English vegetables and produce from their local farm.

Lenka Krepelkova

Visit www.litteraction.org.uk and either join your local group or, if there isn't one, start one up – it's really very easy, and all the information and help that you need is on the website.

George Monck

Put your pledge to do something to change the world on Pledge Bank and get others to do the same. If you need encouragement, go to Stickk.com and define some rewards and punishments for achieving or not achieving your goal, and get a group of friends around you as cheerleaders.
Or as another very simple step, go to www.therainforestsite.com, click, and save one square metre of rainforest - this will cost you nothing.
www.pledgebank.com

Michael Norton

C.A.L.M is the charity I support:
The Campaign Against Living Miserably raises awareness of depression amongst young men: if enough support was given, one day it shouldn't have to be a charity anymore because we would be aware of these potential problems.
www.thecalmzone.net

Philip Levine

Support the various cotton programs that help African farmers farm organically, get their cotton to retailers and new markets, and also add fairtrade premiums which allow them to be self-sufficient.
www.fairtradeafrica.net

Jacqueline Shaw

Only buy things if you know where they've come from. If you aren't sure it wasn't made by a slave then don't buy it.
www.slaveryfootprint.org

Jessi Baker

I've often felt ambivalent about politics; as a young person, I felt politicians were self-serving and didn't appear to care much about the issues that were important to me, and nowadays the things that I get passionate about are community and environmental issues. Try and make a change at a local level. I'm helping campaign for a local adventure playground in my local borough of Tower Hamlets to stay open, for example. Also I applied for a grant to build a small herb and vegetable garden for a local playgroup, and I see toddlers there every day learning how to grow herbs and vegetables. You don't have to be a powerful or wealthy person, you just have to have an idea and the commitment to follow it through.

Tabitha Potts

I have variously supported or worked for different causes including ChildLine, Oxfam, Amnesty International, the Soil Association, Greenpeace and others. But my Vote for this future is Mindapples - the 5-a-day for your mind. It's a campaign working to make looking after our minds as normal as brushing our teeth. My future is one where we treat each other and the world around us well - so we should start with ourselves! Vote by practising your five daily mindapples.
www.mindapples.org

Laura Billings

Get on Twitter. It is becoming the 24/7 vote, the live embodiment of the hive mind. Tech addiction is a growing problem but there is a place for 'Digital Citizenship' – Twitter is the new vote and it is almost becoming a civic duty to get an account.
www.twitter.com

Patrick Hussey

It's easy to get angry. I know that from experience. But I think if we could all turn that anger into action, a lot of people would benefit and it would make you feel better too. Find a charity. Call them up or write to them and offer your time and services. Volunteer. If you don't have enough time for that, visit www.amnesty.org and join, donate, sign a petition every now and then. Or create your own campaign. What and who matters the most to you? Get a pen and paper and start writing down some ideas.

Abrar Agil

I suggest that we simply look after those around us.
I tend to believe that if we all do something at a micro level, then the macro effects will disseminate in a manner that is way more embedded into our culture. The result of that is that it will also feel more rewarding as it will be visible to your eyes, whatever it is.
The idea of choosing a cause can be too loaded.
Before doing that, do something yourself.

Joao Machado

I think bottled water is a waste of consumers' money, a huge polluter (think of the distribution involved) and is detrimental to our health (often, the plastic bottles contain BPAs, which are hugely contentious medically, with links to infertility, depression and other nasties). It's so easy to refill a BPA-free bottle these days, or just drink filtered tap water from a glass, I pledge never to buy another bottle of water again!

Ellie Good

Get involved locally, and work with your neighbours, to create a thriving community. The key to a better society can be found in enhanced community engagement, whereby accountability is created through respect, meaning, ownership and belonging. Moreover, there is much to be gained by volunteering on your doorstep – you can, amongst other things, boost your confidence, create new friendships, enhance your self-worth; and learn new skills, as well as fostering pride in where you live.

Emily Wilkie

Subscribe to the Times. Preferably in print AND online. Failing that, get a Twitter account and follow the 25 people or institutions you resent most.

Oliver Moody

Support scientific progress and like-minded candidates. Don't even talk about the others; don't give them the airtime. Keep religion out of government. Stay informed... Your money is a valuable voting tool. Support good companies. Also, take care of yourself. Don't eat junk. You're one part of a huge, interconnected web. Every action has its consequence.

Max Lugavere

The paradigm shift from More to Better (the organic paradigm) is something that we all can execute every day by "voting with our feet": If we decide to just do something a little bit better every single day the world will be a better place.

Ida Burchardi

There are loads of things we can support to make a better future you know. One is to work with communities like the London recycling network and make sure that nothing goes to waste; to work with long standing charities like Oxfam, who have proven over decades the value that they can achieve on behalf of society; to follow quirky little initiatives like The Uniform Project, where a young lass called Sheena decided she was going to wear the one little black dress for 365 days and style it up a different way every day, and show what can be done with creativity. It was a happy project, it was an intelligent project, it was a creative project, it was a sustainable project all rolled into one.
www.oxfam.org
www.theuniformproject.com

Wayne Hemingway

My Vote goes for Spark & Mettle: they are new charity organisation that are trying to help youths get into their dream career no matter how wacky it may be.
www.sparkandmettle.org.uk

Umair Baig

I really like Do the Green Thing for the interactive videos that inspire sustainable living as well as Junction 49 for providing an effective platform to get young people to initiate their own creative projects.
www.dothegreenthing.com
www.junction49.co.uk

Christina Rebel

Get involved with a newly launched project 'Walked This Earth' that is setting out to capture, educate and inspire a new perspective on intergenerational learning and wisdom.
www.walkedtheearth.wordpress.com

Kate Andrews

Look for the things that are wrong, and just as much
or even more, for the things that should be right.
If no-one's doing anything about it yet, and there's
a chance you could... and really, you can't wait for
someone older or better qualified to do it, because
you might be waiting forever and a day... then do it.
So start a conversation, hoist a flag, spread the word!
You never know what might happen. There'll be failures
and reverses intermingled with joy and success.
But along the way, we'll all learn more and more
about the futures we are choosing and not choosing.

And just as much... join in where other people lead.
If someone else hoisted a flag before you – great!
Thank them. Lend a hand for at least a second if
you can. Sign a petition, join a party, grow a business,
plant a tree. This will take all of us, sharing our hopes
and dreams and projects and dancing together,
toward a better dawn.

Paul Hilder

Rather than support a campaign or donate to a charity, why not pledge to support a person today? Someone that you know who may need some of your time, or someone to champion them, or to listen to them, or to bounce ideas off, to be a comrade. Think of somebody that you believe in, that you think is amazing and ask him or her what you can do for them, but make a commitment to do it for a period of time.

Cassie Robinson

A Vote to create the future I chose is to support and give voice to English PEN and International PEN campaigns, especially the ones concerning imprisoned writers and free expression.
www.pen-international.org

Miguel Fernandes Ceia

Check out Moneythink, the nonprofit organisation I help to run. We're always looking for volunteers, donors, and advocates! We're in the middle of a double-dip recession and, while all the press attention is going to Wall Street and middle America, youth in the urban inner-cities are the ones who have gotten hit the hardest by the financial crisis. By pairing highly trained, highly talented college-age mentors with urban high-schoolers to teach personal finance and facilitate entrepreneurship seminars, Moneythink is educating and activating the next generation of financially responsible consumers and small business leaders. If I didn't think this is one of the best solutions to one of society's biggest problems, I wouldn't be working on it and I wouldn't be making it my Vote.
www.moneythink.org

Ted Gonder

Support The Arts Council so that we continue to promote art in the UK. And at least give the opportunity to people to access art wherever they are in the country.
www.artscouncil.org.uk

Jo Cheung

Encourage your local school to link up with a scientific charity or organisation. You can find them via the Association of Medical Research Charities.
www.amrc.org.uk

Leonor Stjepic

Join Little Episodes, the independent publisher and arts production company that I set up, because I believe that all talent is equal regardless of commercial success. Join the movement as a creative, a person who enjoys the fruits of others' creativity or as a person who cares about others. www.littleepisodes.org

Lucie Barât

Get involved through the existing structures, both local and national, to lobby your representatives. It isn't that sexy but it works. You will be amazed by how much power you actually have. Write to your councillors and your members of parliament – use They Work for You or Write to Them. If you see intolerant or incorrect articles or programmes in the media, contact the Press Complaints Commission or file a petition at e-petitions. www.theyworkforyou.com www.writetothem.com

Dan Snow

I believe that today's parties do not represent the voters, especially the under 30s. This is why we should back smaller parties and get their voices represented in parliament. We could also pledge our allegiance to human rights groups such as BIHR, Liberty and Amnesty International so that people are aware of what is happening around the world.

Iram Ramzan

Join Republic. There is a democratic alternative to the monarchy. www.republic.org.uk

Dave Stuttle

In some ways very trivial, but definitely a tiny, tiny step towards feeling healthier, caring about the environment, and challenging ourselves to be out of our comfort zone: Outdoor Swimming Society. www.outdoorswimmingsociety.com

Alistair Humphreys

I joined both the Labour Party and the Christian Socialist Movement at the same time. I feel that by engaging in politics and social action, I can contribute to society better. You can sign up to the 'big three' political parties at their various websites, and get involved as constituency officers or campus groups.

Jeremy Dillon

This is a hard one to answer; there are so many different ways to help. I recently found out about www.missrepresentation. org which is a website set up to try to get rid of gender stereotypes, and hopefully make a change.

Rubi Anwar

Vote for peace in Congo. Our worlds' deadliest war is currently being fueled and funded by the trading of minerals necessary for electronics. That's right, cell phones, computers etc. Vote for conflict-free phones. Vote for conflict-free everything. Let's make sure our purchases fund a future we choose. One way you can help is to buy and wear a whistle from Falling Whistles. Use it as a symbol of protest and a tool to elevate common conversation. Everywhere you go people will ask about it and it will be your chance to speak up for peace. www.fallingwhilstes.com

Sean Carasso

Defend your tastes. It could be very easy to be shy about enjoying Katy Perry's music when you make your living playing Steve Reich and Benjamin Britten, but there is a reason why it speaks of the time in which we live. Strive to identify relevance in work and we'll start seeing snobbish walls crumble – I'm sure of it.

Peter Gregson

My Vote is literally, to vote. Even if not for your own sake, then for the sake of everyone who has fought and who is still fighting to be given the opportunity to do so.

Eugenie Teasley

Lend money to smart, hard-working entrepreneurs via kiva.org

Graham Hill

Next time you interact with a politician who is asking for your vote or your money, ask them first if they are willing to let you know who is giving them money, who they are meeting with, or if they are willing to legislate that all public information (except security or privacy related) be made available in digital searchable form. If the answer is no, your vote should be too. Sure, governments and politicians have a right and a duty to keep some information secret, and to use discretion when wielding power and diplomacy, but the balance has tipped horribly in the wrong direction.

Currently government information is kept "closed" by default. It should be open by default and, when needed, the government should argue to keep such sensitive information secure. Today we have the opposite situation, where everything the government does is set to closed by default, and we have to argue to release information that as a public we already own. Once we can get the government to open up, then the activities of proprietary industries to influence policy and regulation will be exposed, thus disrupting their monopolies so that a new era of openness can emerge.

To learn more take a look at the work of the Sunlight Foundation, where I am a senior advisor, and you will find a series of tools and initiatives to make our political system open and much more accountable.
www.sunlightfoundation.com

Andrew Rasiej

The future belongs to those that are inspired, who take risks, who push down the barriers of conformity and ignore the pessimists. To those that not only see change but make the change.

Chris Arnold

DIY
FUTURES
INTER-
VIEWS

How Can We Create
The Future You Choose?

Fill in your own Futures Interview
and then ask four of the people
that you respect the most in the
world to share their's in your book.

You may wish to keep your
answers private and share them
only with yourself, your friends
or family. If you want to share
your futures interview with the
global community
and inspire others across
the world, please visit
www.thefutureisbeautiful.co/
futures-interview
where you can add your futures
interview online.

You can download more
interviews online to give to friends
or use in workshops.

My Futures Interview

What is the FUTURE That You Choose?

Your future is the world you want to live in.

What's a THINK to Create this Future?

Your think is something that has informed and inspired the future that you choose.

What's an ACT to Create this Future?

Your act is something that we can all do to help create the future that you choose.

What's a VOTE to Create this Future?

Your vote is a pledge of allegiance to something that you believe is creating the future you choose.

Future Soundtrack – What song will you take with you into the future?

We know, it's an impossibility to pick just one! Add your song to our future soundtrack playlist.

What are your five all time favourite weblinks?

Be part of our directory, with so much to see and do online - what do you think is the most interesting & inspiring?

☐ shared on www.thefutureisbeautiful.co/futures-interview

The Futures Interview

Name   ....

Email   ....

What is the FUTURE That You Choose?

Your future is the world you want to live in.

What's a THINK to Create this Future?

Your think is something that has informed and inspired the future that you choose.

What's an ACT to Create this Future?

Your act is something that we can all do to help create the future that you choose.

What's a VOTE to Create this Future?

Your vote is a pledge of allegiance to something that you believe is creating the future you choose.

Future Soundtrack – What song will you take with you into the future?

We know, it's an impossibility to pick just one! Add your song to our future soundtrack playlist.

What are your five all time favourite weblinks?

Be part of our directory, with so much to see and do online - what do you think is the most interesting & inspiring?

☐ please share this with the global community
☐ shared on www.thefutureisbeautiful.co/futures-interview

The Futures Interview

Name ....
Email ....

What is the FUTURE That You Choose?

Your future is the world you want to live in.

What's a THINK to Create this Future?

Your think is something that has informed and inspired the future that you choose.

What's an ACT to Create this Future?

Your act is something that we can all do to help create the future that you choose.

What's a VOTE to Create this Future?

Your vote is a pledge of allegiance to something that you believe is creating the future you choose.

Future Soundtrack – What song will you take with you into the future?

We know, it's an impossibility to pick just one! Add your song to our future soundtrack playlist.

What are your five all time favourite weblinks?

Be part of our directory, with so much to see and do online - what do you think is the most interesting & inspiring?

☐ please share this with the global community
☐ shared on www.thefutureisbeautiful.co/futures-interview

The Futures Interview

Name ....

Email ....

What is the FUTURE That You Choose?

Your future is the world you want to live in.

What's a THINK to Create this Future?

Your think is something that has informed and inspired the future that you choose.

What's an ACT to Create this Future?

Your act is something that we can all do to help create the future that you choose.

What's a VOTE to Create this Future?

Your vote is a pledge of allegiance to something that you believe is creating the future you choose.

Future Soundtrack – What song will you take with you into the future?

We know, it's an impossibility to pick just one! Add your song to our future soundtrack playlist.

What are your five all time favourite weblinks?

Be part of our directory, with so much to see and do online - what do you think is the most interesting & inspiring?

☐ please share this with the global community
☐ shared on www.thefutureisbeautiful.co/futures-interview

The Futures Interview

Name   ....

Email   ....

What is the FUTURE That You Choose?

Your future is the world you want to live in.

What's a THINK to Create this Future?

Your think is something that has informed and inspired the future that you choose.

What's an ACT to Create this Future?

Your act is something that we can all do to help create the future that you choose.

What's a VOTE to Create this Future?

Your vote is a pledge of allegiance to something that you believe is creating the future you choose.

Future Soundtrack – What song will you take with you into the future?

We know, it's an impossibility to pick just one! Add your song to our future soundtrack playlist.

What are your five all time favourite weblinks?

Be part of our directory, with so much to see and do online - what do you think is the most interesting & inspiring?

☐ please share this with the global community
☐ shared on www.thefutureisbeautiful.co/futures-interview

CREATIVE
ACTIVISM

THE MAKING OF ?!X

Think Act Vote coined the term
Creative Activism:
the act of making something
through art, media or life to create
awareness of and engagement with
important issues of our time
to inspire a brighter future.

'If politics was a fashion brand, you wouldn't wear it.'

Amisha Ghadiali

Think Act Vote (?!X) started with an eco T-shirt design competition and a handmade wooden ballot box. It was born out of a desire to host a new conversation about our future - one with individuals and communities who are often put off by the standard political tone and stances.

We wanted to start a conversation about politics being bigger than Westminster, and in fact something that is around us in every moment, developing the idea that we are constantly thinking, acting and voting through how we spend our time, energy and money.

We brought together creative energy to challenge the negativeperception held by so many in the UK today about both politics and our future. It's a 'Rock the Vote' for the concept of personal agency; politics with a small 'p' if you like, focusing on the future we choose (and can create) through the daily decisions we make.

We began this through creative projects, using a variety of art forms including poetry, fashion, design, illustration and photography.

> The Ballot Box

In the run up to the 2010 election, we asked everyone we met to vote, with their vision of the future that they choose. We needed a ballot box to take to events and festivals with us, and so we asked artist and sculptor Tuba Gursoy to create one.

"I wanted to put a spin on the traditional ballot box and create something that would take Think Act Vote away from political clichés and engage people more creatively. My work is usually kinetic and much larger, so it was interesting to produce something that was small (ish) and static."

Tuba Gursoy - Artist and Sculptor
www.twitter.com/tuba_gursoy

Photography by
Simon Adrians
of tanglephotography.co.uk

Photography by
Tuba Gursoy

Photography by
Amisha Ghadiali

> The Eco T-Shirt

In February of 2010 we searched for the perfect design for our carbon neutral T-shirt from up and coming designers, artists and illustrators. The only proviso was that the design had to include the words 'Think Act Vote.'

The T-shirt produced in partnership with ethical fashion label Komodo serves as a reminder that we can think, act and vote every day to create the future that we choose. The T-shirts were printed onto climate neutral 'EarthPositive' T-shirts (100% organic with 90% lower carbon footprint) by the UK's only organic and carbon neutral T-shirt printer 'TShirt & Sons' using non toxic organic inks certified by the Soil Association.

The winner, Jesson Yip, was chosen by our judging panel which was made up of some of the best-known faces in ethical fashion and design, including ethical hero Katharine Hamnett, celebrated illustrator Daisy de Villeneuve and the original 'anti-preneur,' Cyndi Rhoades.

The concept was then developed further by Jesson Yip and the Komodo Design team, with different colour versions for male and female. The different fonts used within the symbols represent different voices within society.

"The idea for the design came in the early sketches. It was the one that really stuck out and I loved how the three actions could all be represented by typographic symbols. The design stands out as something a bit different; the hope is that it will create intrigue and spark off a conversation or two."

Jesson Yip

Artwork by
Holly Berry

Photography by
Ben Gold

www.tshirtandsons.co.uk
www.earthpositiveapparel.com

Original Think Act Vote competition artwork by Holly Berry:
Textile Designer and Illustrator
www.hollyberryprojects.com

Design Competition Winner – Jesson Yip:
Digital and Interaction Designer
www.jessonyip.com

T-Shirt Competition Judges:
Katharine Hamnett: Ethical Fashion Designer and Campaigner
www.katharinehamnett.com
Daisy de Villeneuve: Illustrator and Designer
www.daisydevilleneuve.com
Cyndi Rhoades: Up-cycler and Entrepreneur
www.wornagain.co.uk

Joe Komodo: Fashion Designer and Author
www.komodo.co.uk
Peter Hames: Entrepreneur
www.sleepio.com
Jocelyn Whipple: Sustainable Fabrics Expert
www.element23.co.uk
Rosie Budhani: PR and Media Specialist
www.foundation-agency.com
Amisha Ghadiali: Ethical Jewellery Designer nd Activist
www.amisha.co.uk
T-shirt Sponsor, Komodo: Organic and Fair Trade fashion brand since 1988
www.komodo.co.uk

> ?!X Refashioned

We gave T-shirts to some of the leading ethical fashion brands in London - to customize the simple T-shirt into a unique piece. Eight designers took part: Junky Styling, Ada Zanditon, Beautiful Soul, Traid Remade, Nancy Dee, Ciel, Tara Starlet, and Miksani ... each giving a different twist to the ?!X tee. The brief was to use just a T-shirt and offcuts from previous collections (that might have otherwise been thrown away) to create the pieces. We gave them just a week to do it, and couldn't believe how stunning what we got back was. Some designers opted to create more of a showpiece in a signature style, and others chose to create something that can be made at home, giving instructions how to do it.

Photography by Dominic Clarke dominicclarke.com
Ethically Styled by Io Takemura iotakemura.com

Showpieces

Nancy Dee

Nancy Dee is an ethical womenswear label specialising in day-to-night jersey. Nancy Dee creates stylish, versatile pieces that translate easily from home to office to an evening out. Nancy Dee is run by sisters Tamsin and Seraphina Davis. "The showpiece is based on one of Nancy Dee's most popular designs that combine a cute mini-dress with a contrasting T-shirt top. The look reflects Nancy Dee's colourful and retro style. The original T-shirt was recycled to avoid wastage of fabric - as is evident from the design element of the two circular cut-outs. The additional fabric was added from their current Spring/Summer collection - a fabulous jersey mix of sustainable soybean and organic cotton. Soybean is a fantastic fibre for fabric, as it is recycled from the waste of other soy products like tofu and soya milk. When spun and knitted with organic cotton, it becomes a super-soft, drapey jersey." Seraphina Davis

www.thefutureisbeautiful.co/2010/06/25/nancydee
www.nancydee.co.uk

Dress by Nancy Dee , **Scarf by** Tamasyn Gambell

TRAIDremade

TRAIDremade specialises in turning damaged textiles, vintage items and clothing destined for landfill into gorgeous clothes and accessories. Set up in 2002 by fashion recycling charity TRAID, the label was conceived as a way to create beautiful clothing from waste.

"I created an asymmetric look and combined it with stretch jersey. The jersey was taken from five shop-soiled sweaters. I took each one apart and then re-stitched the panels together to create a piece of fabric to cut a pattern from. Finally, the front panel of the dress was created by incorporating the 'THINK, ACT, VOTE' Tee.'
– Paula Kirkwood, Designer at TRAID Remade

www.thefutureisbeautiful.co/2010/07/15/think-act-vote-refashioned-traidremade
www.traid.org.uk
www.traidremade.com

Dress by Traid Remade, **Leggings by** Ivana Helsinki, **Shoes by** Terra Plana

Junky Styling

Junky Styling is an innovative design-led label. All garments are made from the highest quality secondhand clothing, which is deconstructed, re-cut and completely transformed.

Designers Annika Sander and Kerry Seager want to 'transform something simple and a bit masculine into something flirty and feminine.'

www.thefutureisbeautiful.co/2010/07/21/junky-styling
www.junkystyling.co.uk

Dress by Junky Styling, **Necklace by** Amisha Elegance Rebellion, **Shoes by** Terra Plana

Ada Zanditon

Ada Zanditon is an award winning designer. The vision of her brand is to create elegant, sculptural womenswear embellished with Zanditon's original illustrations. The silhouettes are strong, confident and geometrically cut, featuring origami inspired, engineered details.

Dress by Ada Zanditon, **Ring & Head Accessory by** Amisha Elegance Rebellion, **Shoes by** Beyond Skin

'The first idea I had was very pop art and very literal.' She decided to make ballot boxes and sew them onto the T-shirt. 'But just at that time, sadly, Malcolm McLaren died. He was a huge inspiration to me when I was younger; I think that he was an incredibly provocative person and what he instigated caused people to completely re-think, re-evaluate. It hugely encouraged people to think, without reverence for a system, but actually about everything. He really altered people's perception of music, art and politics. So I was looking at the pictures in one of my favourite books, England's Dreaming, and I wanted to make a pretty straightforward tribute to Punk, to him and to its place in the British, psyche of provocation, action, short thinking and acting – and taking decisions based on independent, individual thoughts.'

www.thefutureisbeautiful.co/2010/07/12/think-act-vote-refashioned-ada-zandition
www.adazanditon.com

Beautiful Soul

Beautiful Soul is a British luxury womenswear label created by Nicola Woods. The label's signature is a blend of timeless evolving style with true global consideration. Quintessentially English with a wholly international appeal, it is a fresh and innovative label that emits sophistication.

'Women these days aren't taken in by throwaway fashion, and seek to buy and wear clothes that are unique and timeless. The use of a vintage Japanese kimono offers exclusivity and, by giving it a new lease of life, it is hoped that it can be cherished for a lifetime. We have captured Beautiful Soul's signature style, but have also added a playful twist, in keeping with the refreshing message of Think Act Vote.

The collar is removable and has been made from old business cards (that were produced in error) and combined with scraps of organic peace silk, providing a solution to 'zero' waste. The garment is multifunctional and can be worn as a dress or as a skirt, depending on your mood; after all, a woman loves to change her mind!' Nicola Woods

www.thefutureisbeautiful.co/2010/07/06/think-act-vote-refashioned-beautiful-soul
www.beautiful-soul.co.uk

Complete Look by Nicola Woods, Beautiful Soul

Tara Starlet

Tara Starlet is a vintage inspired fashion line with responsible ethics and a timeless charm. Created and run by a mother and daughter team, Tara Starlet is a family business, born out of a shared passion for the glory days of the 1940s and 50s, and a mutual concern for the wellbeing of our planet and its inhabitants.

'When tackling the challenge of upcycling the Think Act Vote T-shirt, it was a no brainer that I would have to make it into a dress. I chose to do a fluted skirt because I wanted it to be a nice classic 40s length and I didn't just want to attach a skirt onto a waistband.

www.thefutureisbeautiful.co/2010/07/13/think-act-vote-refashioned-tara-starlet
www.tarastarlet.com

The fabric I used was scrap from some blouses we have made in the past. Making a fluted skirt out of panels meant that I could create the effect of something that would take a lot of fabric to make, using scrap pieces sewn together.' Tara Scott

Dress by Tara Starlet, **Bangles by** Amisha Elegance Rebellion

Customisations

Ciel

Ciel is an award winning, pioneering eco-philosophy designer fashion brand, created by Sarah Ratty.

'I wanted to create something that didn't need a sewing machine and which anyone with a good pair of fabric scissors could re-create.' Sarah Ratty

T-shirt and Scarf by Ciel, **Skirt by** Lu Flux,
Shoes by Terra Plana Necklace,
Bangles by Amisha Elegance Rebellion

Sarah Ratty tells us how to make the EcoChic Think Act Vote Ciel top at home:

1. Take 2 x Think Act Vote Organic t-shirts 1 x womens, 1 x mens

2. Then cut the neckline off to create a wide boat neck and cut a vertical line down the centre back of the large men's tee and open it out.

3. Cut a large curved right angle from the centre front of the tee, to make the scarf shape, then fold it in half to make a template and a mirror cut to replicate the first shape. Add long tails at the top to create neckties with.

4. Tie a knot in each necktie piece about 20 cm to create the shape.

5. Next fold the raw outside edges by 1cm to make a seam allowance and make several small vertical cuts to make holes for neckties.

6. From the waste cut several 10cm bias strips & loop them through the holes & tie in place onto one side of the V front of scarf to create the tassels.

7. Cut three long wide bias strips from the remaining waste and plait them through the opposite side of the V front.

8. Take the women's tee and lay it flat on the table and cut a curved line from the under arm up to the shoulder seam.

9. Fix the two pieces together and assemble them to make the final piece!

www.thefutureisbeautiful.co/2010/07/22/think-act-vote-refashioned-ciel

www.cielshop.co.uk

Miksani

Miksani create stylish, luxury fashion whilst employing socially responsible and ethical business practices. The garments are manufactured to the highest standards in Nepal, Peru and India, using natural, sustainable fabrics such as organic cotton and silk, banana, alpaca wool and mohair wool.

'I used an old white T-shirt the same size as the T.A.V. tee. Using as much fabric from the t-shirt as possible, I created fringes by slicing the fabric into strips and then stretching them out to create tubes. I then cut the T.A.V. T-shirt up both sides and stitched in the fringed sections to create the T-shirt. I wanted to create something contemporary that would be fairly easy for anyone to re-create, with the added material being something that most people may have lying around.' Katie Weightman, Designer at Miksani.

The process to create your own Miksani customization of the T-shirt has been illustrated below in 9 easy steps:

1. Get an old top the same size as your Think Act Vote t-shirt.
2. Mark out lines with chalk going down from the shoulder seams to the bottom.
3. Cut your old t-shirt straight down in the middle.
4. Cut off the sleeve and down the side edge of the old t-shirt.
5. Cut these panels into strips 1cm wide, leaving 2cm uncut down the edge.
6. Stretch out these strips (they will automatically go into 'tubes').
7. Cut your Think Act Vote t-shirt up both the sides you have marked.
8. Trap the fringing into the front, back and both sides of your Think Act Vote t-shirt and stitch (so the stitching shows on the inside of the t-shirt).
9. Your t-shirt is done.

www.thefutureisbeautiful.co/2010/06/24/miksani
www.miksani.com

T-shirt by Miksani, **Jacket by** Junky Styling, **Trousers** by Ada Zanditon

>?!X Photobooth

We took the ?!X photobooth around the UK to festivals and events, creating conversations about the future. The people we met were invited to have their photograph taken in one of our eco T-shirts or ?!X refashioned pieces.

Photography Credits:
this page
Amisha Ghadiali
www.amisha.co.uk
Poulomi Basu
www.poulomibasu.com

next page
Maciej Groman
www.mgroman.co.uk
James Wicks
www.jameswicksphoto.com
Ludovic des Cognets
www.ldescognets.com

page 168
Ludovic des Cognets
ldescognets.com

page 169
Vanya Sacha
vanyasacha.com

previous page
Vanya Sacha
vanyasacha.com
Marcia Chandra
marciachandra.com

this page
Deven
flickr.com/photos/capikon
Ben Gold
bengold.co.uk
Poulomi Basu
poulomibasu.com
Deepti V. Patel
deeptivijaypatel.co.uk
James Wicks
jameswicksphoto.com
Pip Dudrah
pipdudrah.com

To view all of the photographs online and to tag yourself or people you know,
visit www.thefutureisbeautiful.co/ecofashion/photobooth

>The Poetry Competition

The night before the 2010 general election we announced the winner of The Future I Choose poetry competition that was judged by wordsmiths John Bird, Founder of The Big Issue, and Shane Solanki, Writer and Performer.

The Runners-up:

Think Act Vote by Paul Williamson

What difference can one person make,
Which route can someone willing take?
Sometimes big things cause procrastination,
Take small steps towards the destination,
Pick a path then set off walking,
Choose a viewpoint and get talking,
Actions speak much louder than words,
But pick for yourself, avoid the herds,
Groups of people can get things done,
But every collective begins with one,
Stand up and be counted,
Think it out, act wisely, and vote.

The Future I Choose by Richard Watkins

It's not universally acceptable to say how much you enjoy things,
Much more popular to point at problems -
Proclaim precisely when and where we got downtrodden.
But friends can be frank so let us speak candidly:
We all have more cause to thank than cause to panic.
And our calamities, although inconvenient, are rarely titanic.
So – what shall we do with this habitual imbalance in our speech?
Well, it hardly requires a grand intellectual leap.
Maybe we just need to give nice things more attention,
A mention at least.

The Winner:

The Happiness Project by Olivia Sprinkel

I seize upon the pink stickie,
On the community workshop wall.
'Happiness Project'. Let's create it.
Let's do, do, do, let's plan a project,
Let's make it happen, let's take those
Five or seven steps to happiness.
This is my happiness project.
This cardboard cup of soup,
Celeriac and pear, paler than
The winter sun. The warmth
Of the pot soft as a lover's hand.
I dip my spoon. It sails out to sea.
The sweetness of a radiant autumn
Afternoon, pressing chunks of
Red apple and green pear plucked
From a blue sky, dripping juice.
The earthiness of a kitchen evening,
A heavy pan of celeriac gratin,
Bubbling browned from the oven,
Melt of cream and molten laughter.
This is my happiness project,
Contained here in this cup of soup.
I look out, pull my scarf tighter, watch
A pink-booted pigeon parade
On the glass palisade, whilst the river
Washes scudding clouds away.

>The Futures Interview

After over a year of asking people to vote with the visions of the future that they choose, we decided to expand our questions by introducing the Futures Interview. Through our Thinks, Acts and Votes we can create the future we choose.

Future Interview doodles by Lauren Currie, www.redjotter.wordpress.com

>The ?!X Manifesto

In October 2011 we were asked to write a manifesto for the Hub's 1000 Changemakers Project. Our original manifesto was hand illustrated by artist Robert Reed and the poster was hung on the wall at the Hub Westminster. www.thisisreed.com

Every second the world is changing, and we shape it by how we spend our time, money and energy. WE THINK, ACT AND VOTE. WE CREATE THE FUTURE WE CHOOSE. This is how we express our power and our voice. We can't create it if we don't know what we want, and **every one of us has ideas and experiences** that can lead us to a better world. We need to make space to see the world as it is now, and as it could be, and share our collective vision of the future. We must resist the temptation to put people and things in boxes, but instead **listen and learn**. We know that everything is connected, so we work across boundaries, difference, industries and personalities. We **understand our values** and we bring them into everything that we do. We don't have all the answers and so we ask everybody these questions: What is the **FUTURE** That You Choose? Your Future is the world you want to live in. What's a **THINK** to Create this Future? Your Think is something that has **informed and inspired** the future that you choose. What's an **ACT** to Create this Future? Your Act is something that **we can all do to help** create the future that you choose. What's a **VOTE** to Create this Future? Your Vote is a **pledge of allegiance** to something that you believe is creating the future you choose. If we can answer these questions individually, then collectively we can **build our shared future, together.** The Future I Choose is the Future I never even thought of – before **each one of you** opened my eyes.

Think Act Vote Manifesto

? ! X
THINK ACT VOTE

175

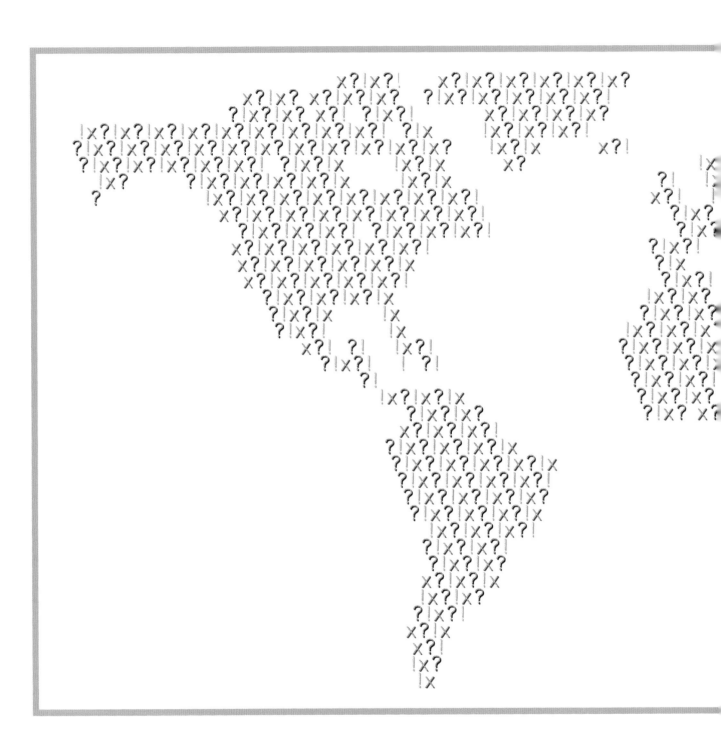

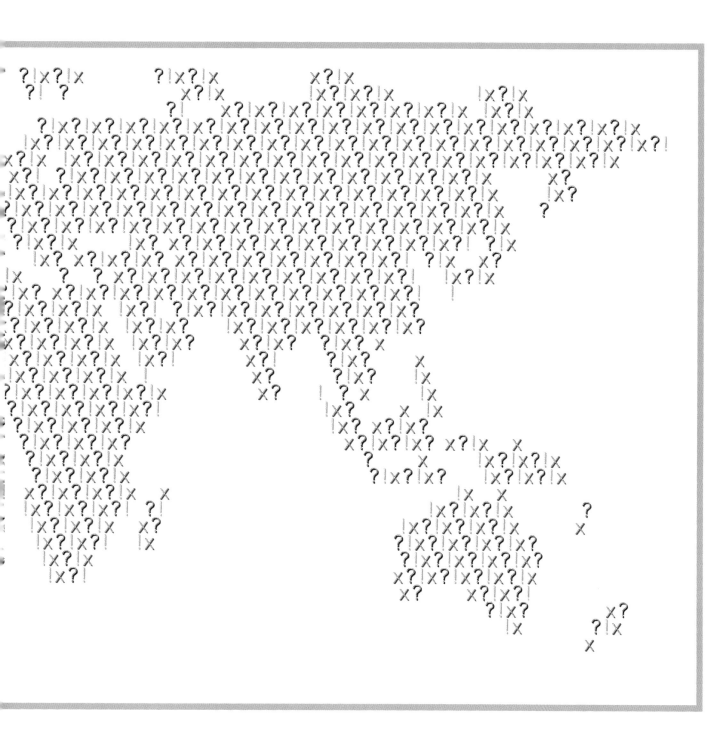

Think Act Vote Manifesto artwork and map by Deniz Tekkul- www.deniztekkul.com

>Futures Illustration

In late 2011, we selected 52 of the most powerful Futures we had received in our ballot box, and created an open brief for artists to come forward and select a future to bring to life.

1

Dominic Campbell's Future "is one where we stand together for justice and what is right, where everyone is given the freedom and opportunity to dream and make those dreams a reality."

Artwork by Thom Lambert:
"I chose to illustrate Dominic Campbell's future because it is a sentiment I really related to. Dreams have always been a driving force in my life, something to aim for and hopefully, achieve. I think people are too quick to dismiss others' dreams and it's a shame because these ideas and ambitions can really grow into something special, if allowed to. Being able to stand together for justice is something that should happen more often than it does. I think this goes hand in hand with freedom of speech. My artwork was intended to be a very loose, almost spontaneous stylistic interpretation of this, with a smile of broken chains to represent freedom of speech and then the ideas flowing freely from the mind of the character portrayed."
thomlambert.com

2

Jocelyn Whipple's "is one where all our resources and energy are renewable and sustainable. By investing in clean and truly renewable technology and ways of working, we all have the capacity to envision and participate in a less doom-ridden future. I look forward to this future where ownership wars for finite resources are left behind, making way for more positive developments in human culture."

Artwork by Abi Daker:
"I chose this future because the issue of sustainable energy is one I feel particularly strongly about. I live in a house with solar panels and they are such an effective energy source and we have found it perfectly possible to adapt our lifestyles to any of the inconsistencies in hot water production etc. I've never found wind turbines to be anything other than an attractive sight, either, so I decided to base my illustration around showing the turbines in a beautiful and positive way. I based the illustration around mid-20th century travel poster art."
abidaker.com

3

Wayne Hemingway's Future "is fitter, healthier, happier, less greedy, more liveable, more equal and beautifully designed."

Artwork by Natalia Nazimek:
"I chose this one because Hemingway perfectly described the kind of world I want to live in. My main inspiration was nature and positive emotions. I've tried to show that we can build this amazing, colorful future if we want to."
nthlee.tumblr.com

4

Orsola de Castro's Future where "we are collectively trying to shape a new future, less about greed, more about understanding."

Artwork by Luke Waller
"I was inspired to choose Orsola de Castro's future because of its simplicity and direct message. It says all it needs to about the current climate and how we can all help to change it."
lukewaller.co.uk

5

David de Rothschild's Future "is one where today we all dare to dream bigger, undertake greater adventures, tell richer stories and strive to be more curious thereby collectively solving the issues that we know the future will hold."

Artwork by Kirstie Battson:
"I chose David de Rothchild's future as it encompasses positive ideals of change – encouraging us to dream, seek out new experiences, and explore. In the current economic climate, where it can be hard to find time for oneself and stay hopeful, it's nice to imagine a future where one can be productive and excited about what may come. I used this notion of productivity to help create my image; with pencils, buildings, and trees representing creativity, growth, and constructive change respectively in our future. The whole notion itself is still depicted as a dream however, as this future isn't yet a certainty – it is something that we must shape and nurture."

heykirstie.co.uk

7

Jameela Oberma's Future "is one where Young people are inspired, not apathetic and cynical, and are believers in their power to cause positive and political reform."

Artwork by Nanae Kawahara:
"I am not one to act aggressively. I was inspired by Miss Oberma's 'and are believers in their power to cause positive and political reform'. I think people do not need to have extreme actions. However, they need to have their thoughts, obviously. There should be a lot of colours and forms. I included them in my illustration work for this project as they are the ideas of many people. Although this might not be apparent at first, like mixed forms in my work, I believe that will come to be finally formed."

barbaratics.com

6

Anna Murray's Future is one "where people are more sensitive to their surroundings, instead of constantly hurrying from A to B, and are living in greater harmony with the everyday."

Artwork by Katie Harnett:
"I chose to illustrate Anna Murray's future as I think the idea of a harmonious coexistence with our surroundings is fundamental in achieving a sustainable future. Hopefully as we become more sensitive to our surroundings we will take better care of them, and appreciate more the importance of preserving natural resources. I also liked the idea of a more leisurely, less harried way of life, and tried to portray this in my illustration, by presenting both the negative 'constantly hurrying' lifestyle and a more relaxed, harmonious one. "

cargocollective.com/katieharnett

8

Chris Lonie's Future" is one where young people are as keen to vote for politicians as they are for X-factor contestants."

Artwork by Antonia Parker:
"I chose to illustrate Chris Lonie's future...because I work with a lot of young people. The X-factor really seems to capture their imagination and they get very passionate about following their favourite (or not-so favourite!) acts through the process. The rigmarole and the hype in the run-up to general elections is so very similar, I wonder why they aren't as inspired by their political candidates. Perhaps because the voting age doesn't extend to them, they feel it isn't relevant. It was an interesting development when the Leaders Debate was televised for the first time during the 2010 General Election, but I felt surprised it hadn't been done before. For my illustration, I decided that if we want younger people and first-time voters to be more excited about following the election process, we need to directly lift the X Factor format, featuring them as slightly less polished judges deciding the fate of the candidates against the backdrop of the expectation, booming voiceovers and flashy graphics of the show."

antoniamakes.com

179

1

A FUTURE

WHERE ALL RESOURCES AND ENERGY
ARE RENEWABLE AND SUSTAINABLE

2

3

4

6

7

1

Josie Nicholson's Future "is one of inclusion, coherence, diversity and community values between people both globally and locally."

Artwork by Ailish Sullivan:
"My illustration tries to mix patterns from lots of different nations from around the world and interlock them. I chose the quote because I have lived in two different countries and know the importance of feeling included as well as the importance of diversity. I hope it conveys a sense that variety can work together and create something more."
ailishillustrations.4ormat.com

2

Amisha Ghadiali's Future is one that "is driven by love and respect, not fear and greed. We'll all be on the same side and working together in support of each other. We'll be using our creative energy to solve the world's problems and we'll be having fun whilst we're doing it. The future I choose is one where it is sexy and cool to care about the planet and its people."

Artwork by Vicky Fallon:
"I chose Amisha's future as I felt automatically drawn to it – creatively and personally. This is where my inspiration came from. I created two girls on each side of the world to represent how we need to support one another and work together. Showing them painting was my interpretation of how we can solve this with our creative energies whilst having fun! Amisha outlined her future so well in just a few words; I aimed to create the same in my artwork in a clear, bold and exciting way."
Vickyink.com

3

Jo Royle's Future "is one where the barriers between nature and societies are blurred, one where we all think of ourselves as environmentalists, as the environment is our umbilical cord for life; and therefore a world where we fulfil our role as caretakers of the planet."

Artwork by Gilly Rochester:
"The nurturing and protective ideas in Jo Royle's future appealed to me, and I liked that her stance allowed for both large and small scale initiatives - combined community efforts but also actions on an individual basis. In the illustration I have tried to respond to Jo's suggestion of both balance and tension between us and our planet – we occupy, appreciate and utilize it, but also abuse, exploit and destroy it. The idea that we nurture the planet like a child in the womb is hopefully balanced with the truth that the Earth is much more important to us than we are to it! I wanted the figure to seem both an ordinary woman and maybe an ethereal being (non-religious!) blessing the Earth. The harlequin/jester and theatre curtain touches were included to give an 'all the world's a stage' element – where we 'ThinkActVote'. I wanted to include some some details like plants and animals and was quite pleased that, by chance I have to confess, it ended up with both farmed and wild animals – the geese."
gillyrochester.com

4

Louie Louie Herbert's Future "is a world with less shoes and more views on things that matter and have beauty."

Artwork by Erica Sharp:
"I chose Louie Louie Herbert's quote as the share of resources in the world is so unbalanced. We in the West have so much, yet demand more and more regardless of its environmental or social impact on our planet and its people. It only takes a look into how the poorest people in our world live, that the next pair of shoes or newest fashion trend just seems so trivial and insignificant. I chose to draw a couple looking upon things which have importance, beauty and power- things that we can think about and change, to make a happier, more resourceful, meaningful future. "
ericasharp.co.uk

5

Justice Williams' Future "is one where creative talent and resources are utilised to close the widening gap between the rich and the poor. Where diversity transcends from a tick box and unites people in celebrating difference.

A future where young and old are given equality of opportunity and social capital is this and next season's new trend. It is a time where being great and celebrating the success of those from tomorrow is embraced, enjoyed and unleashed. The future I choose is one where we say I am proud to be a part of that."

Artwork by Sandhya Garg:
"I chose Justice William's future. My illustration style is full of colors and each color for me has a character. My work here represents the rich by the color purple (purple being associated with royalty); and poor by the colour red (I see it as the colour of the blood that poor people put into their work) ... then merging the two colours together, mingling and intersecting so as to form a world of equal opportunity."
showtime.arts.ac.uk/SandhyaGarg

6
Noel Hatch's Future "is a Glastopolitics, where groups can work together where they feel most comfortable, whether that's on the fringes or on the main stage."

Artwork by Kellie Black/Miss Pearl Grey:
"I chose to illustrate Noel's quote because the description of his future was so evocative; I could see the image that I wanted to create in my mind's eye as soon as I read it. I am a big fan of capturing personalities, and the festival scene that I was inspired to create gave me the perfect opportunity to do this! I loved Noel's idea of lots of characters from all different walks of life coming together in a forum for the greater good, and to me the idea of a Glastonbury style festival seemed like a really exciting way of meshing all of these different characters together."
misspearlgrey.com

7
Katharine Hamnett's Future is one "where we have the dictionary definition of democracy, government by the people, for the people and tolerating minority views."

Artwork by Faye West:
"Hamnett's future really rang true for me. I have no faith in our Government or many other countries' Government for that matter. They do not seem to ever act in the interest of everyday people, or listen to them. I wanted a figure in my illustration that represented Democracy; like the Statue of Liberty, or Justice, reminds us of a value. I also wanted a nod to Hamnett's slogan T-shirts and say something about there being too much emphasis on which party is in power."
fayewest.com

8
Nicola Harwood's Future "is one where everyone knows how to use their voice in their community, or globally."

Artwork by Natalie Hughes:
"This statement resonated to me because as someone who isn't naturally 'political' I think it's important that anyone and everyone is able to express their thoughts on the future of our world. I tried to illustrate the idea that everyone has their own vision of the future, and that in fact there are multiple and endless possibilities for our world. Whatever our future, we should all have our voices heard. I imagined all these voices -all individuals and all with equal importance- and felt comforted that no matter what issues we all face, we live in an age wh ere we can ALL discuss, debate and share our thoughts."
nataliehughes.co.uk

9
Shibin Vasudevan's Future is one "where the word waste ceases to exist in our dictionaries."

Artwork by Maria Papadimitriou:
"The future described by Shibin Vasudevan was one of my favourites as, being a jewellery designer who makes pieces out of what others consider as waste, I feel very strongly about this future being a real possibility if we use our imagination. I have a soft spot for hats and so quite often my illustrations feature headwear..."
slowlytheeggs.com

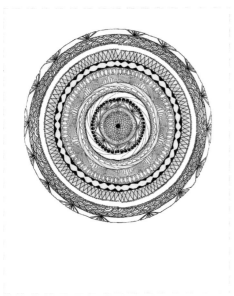

1

2

3 & 4

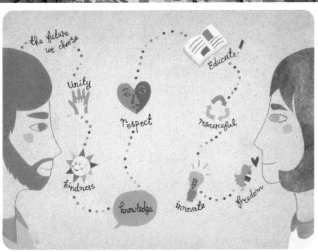

5

6

7

8

9

Throughout 2012 we have been sharing an illustration a week online, as part of our Futures Calendar at www.thefutureisbeautiful.co

Think Act Vote Illustrators:

Abby Wright
abbywrightillustration.co.uk
Abi Daker
abidaker.com
Ailish Sullivan
ailishillustrations.4ormat.com
Alison Day
alisonday.nl
Amber Cassidy
ambercassidy.co.uk
Anila Babla
papersoul.co.uk
Antonia Parker
antoniamakes.com
Bryony Crane
illustration.bryonycrane.me.uk
Celine Elliott
drawingsofpeopleandthings.blogspot.com
Claire Biddles
clairebiddles.com
Claire Kearns
curlyc.co.uk
David Lawrence
davidlawrenceillustration.blogspot.com/2011/09/portfolio.html
Dionisia Tzavalas
dionisiatzavalas.blogspot.co.uk
Elli Chortara
ellichortara.com
Emily Wilkinson
mindfulmaps.com
Emmeline Pidgen
emmelineillustration.com
Erica Sharp
ericasharp.co.uk
Faye West
fayewest.com
Gareth Barnes
garethbarnes.com
Gemma Sheldrake
wix.com/petitecreme/gallery
Gilly Rochester
gillyrochester.com
Harriet Gray
harrietgray.co.uk
Jenny Draw
jenillustration.com
Jenny Robins
jennyrobins.co.uk
Jo Cheung
jocheung.com

Joana Casaca Lemos
joanacasacalemos.com
June Chanpoomidole/ June Sees
junesees.com
Katie Harnett
cargocollective.com/katieharnett
Kellee Rich
kelleerich.com
Kellie Black/ Miss Pearl Grey
misspearlgrey.com
Kiran Patel / Illustrating Rain
cargocollective/illustratingrain
Kirstie Battson/ 'Hey Kirstie'
heykirstie.co.uk
Laura Anderson
lauraellenanderson.co.uk
Laura Frame
lauraframe.co.uk
Lily Freeston
lilianthings.blogspot.com
Luke Waller
lukewaller.co.uk
Maria Papadimitriou / Slowly The Eggs
slowlytheeggs.com
Matthew Dale
matthewgdale.com
Michelle Urval
michelleurvallnyren.com
Mike Harman
mikeharmanillustration.blogspot.com
Nanae Kawahara
barbaratics.com
Natalia Nazimek
nthlee.tumblr.com
Natalie Hughes
nataliehughes.co.uk
Rhea Babla
rheabablaillustration.blogspot.com
Rubi Anwar
the-creative-den.posterous.com
Sam Parr
cargocollective.com/samparr
Sandhya Garg
showtime.arts.ac.uk/SandhyaGarg
Thom Lambert
thomlambert.com
Vicky Fallon
vickyjanefallon.com
Yelena Bryksenkova
yelenabryksenkova.com

>The Future Is Beautiful Visualisation

This meditation recorded by Amisha Ghadiaili takes you through a process of connecting to yourself and visioning the future that you choose. You can download it at www.thefutureisbeautiful.co/meditation

Weblink Directory

We asked contributors to share what they find most interesting and inspiring from around the web. To access this directory online visit www.thefutureisbeautiful.co/weblinks-directory

0

10:10 Global — 1010global.org
365 project — 365project.org
365act — 365act.com
38 Degrees — 38degrees.org.uk
43 Things — 43things.com
826 Valencia — 826valencia.org

A

A Good Week — agoodweek.com
ABCD Europe — abcdeurope.ning.com
Above Magazine — abovemagazine.com
Abundant Community — abundantcommunity.com
Abundant Life Ministries — alm.org.uk
Access Radio — accessradio.biz
Access:Wind — access-wind.com
Aesop's Fables — aesops-fables.org.uk
African Digital Art — africandigitalart.com
Alistair Humphreys — alastairhumphreys.com
Amelia's Magazine — ameliasmagazine.com
Art House Co-op — arthousecoop.com
ArtBelow — artbelow.org.uk
Arts Council — artscouncil.org.uk
Arts Thread — artsthread.co.uk
Association of Medical Research Charities — amrc.org.uk
Avaaz — avaaz.org

B

Bad Science — badscience.net
Bank of Imagination — bankofimagination.com
Battle of Ideas — battleofideas.org.uk
BBC iPlayer — bbc.co.uk/iplayer/radio
BBC Mancunia — stringsta.com/bbcmancunia
BBC News — bbc.co.uk/news
BBC 6music — bbc.co.uk/6music
Beautiful Decay — beautifuldecay.com/about
Before i die — beforeidie.cc
Behance network — behance.net
BEING — being-ldn.com
Ben Casnocha's Blog — casnocha.com/blog
Big Dance 2010 — bigdance2012.com

Big Think	bigthink.com
Bionic Learning Network	festo.com/cms/en_corp 9645.htm
Bjork	bjork.com
Book Cover Archive	bookcoverarchive.com
Boooooooom	boooooooom.com
Brain Pickings	brainpickings.org
Brand Republic	brandrepublic.com/home
Braziliality	braziliality.org
British Inspiration Trust	britishinspirationtrust.org.uk
Brittney Lee	britsketch.blogspot.com
Bruce Lipton	brucelipton.com
Burning Man	burningman.com
Build Africa	build-africa.org
Buzz Bnk	buzzbnk.org

C

Cabbages and Roses	cabbagesandroses.com
CALM	thecalmzone.net
Campaign Against the Arms Trade	caat.org.uk
Canvas8	canvas8.com
Cap Money	capmoney.org
Catalan Cooking	catalancooking.co.uk
Ceasefire magazine	ceasefiremagazine.co.uk
Centre Commercial	centrecommercial.cc
Change.org	change.org
Charley Harper	charleyharperprints.com
Choolips	choolips.com
Christians in Parliament	christiansinparliament.org.uk
Climate Rush	climaterush.co.uk
Code Year	codeyear.com
Colorlines	colorlines.com
Cool Earth	coolearth.org
Copenhagen Design Week	copenhagendesignweek.com
Community Lovers Guide	communityloversguide.org
Corporation 20/20	corporation2020.org
Creativist Society	creativistsociety.com
Cultures of Resistance	culturesofresistance.org
Culture Wars	culturewars.org.uk
Curators of culture	curatorsofculture.com

D

Daily Good	dailygood.org
Daisy Green Magazine	daisygreenmagazine.co.uk
Dalston Farm Shop	farmlondon.weebly.com
Daniel Pearl Foundation	danielpearl.org
Dear Photograph	dearphotograph.com
Democracy Now!	democracynow.org
Derek Sivers' Book Reviews	sivers.org/book
Design Council	designcouncil.org.uk
Design spiration	designspiration.net
Design*Sponge	designsponge.com
DIS	dismagazine.com
Discogs	discogs.com
Ditto.tv	ditto.tv
Do Lectures	dolectures.com
Do the Green Thing	dothegreenthing.com
Do-It	do-it.org.uk
Dropping Knowledge	droppingknowledge.org

E

Earth 2 Hub	earth2channel.com
Easy Fundraising	easyfundraising.co.uk
Ebay	ebay.co.uk
Ecco*eco	eccoeco.blogspot.com
Eckhart Tolle	eckharttolletv.com
Eco Age Blog	eco-age.com
EggMag	eggmag.co.uk
Ekklesia	ekklesia.co.uk
Elephant Family	elephantfamily.org
Elephant Journal	elephantjournal.com
ENCA (Environmental Network for Central America)	enca.org.uk
Energy In Common	energyincommon.org
Energy Share	energyshare.com
Enough is Enough	enough.org
Ethical Fashion Forum	ethicalfashionforum.com
Etsy	etsy.com

F

Fairtrade Foundation	fairtrade.org.uk
Fairshare Music	fairsharemusic.com
Fairtrade Africa	fairtradeafrica.net
Fashioning Change	fashioningchange.com
Fawcett Society	fawcettsociety.org.uk
Feeding the 5k	feeding5k.org
Figment	figment.com
Finisterre	finisterreuk.com
Forum for The Future	forumforthefuture.org
Foundation for Democracy and Sustainable Development	fdsd.org
Free Barbar Ahmed	freebabarahmad.com
Freedom from Torture	torturecare.org.uk
Fresh2o	fresh2o.org
Freedom Theatre	thefreedomtheatre.org
Frontal cortex	wired.com/wiredscience frontal-cortex
Funny Women	funnywomen.com
FutureGov	wearefuturegov.com
FutureVersity	futureversity.org

G

Gary Younge	garyyounge.com
Get A Life	activeresistance.co.uk
Global Oneness Project	globalonenessproject.org
GOOD	good.is
Good for Nothing	goodfornothing.co
Google	google.com
Google Scholar	scholar.google.co.uk
Greenbelt Movement	greenbeltmovement.org
Greenpeace International	greenpeace.org
Guerrilla Gardening	guerrillagardening.org

H

Half Bakery	halfbakery.com
Harvard Business Review	hbr.org

M

N

O

P

Pledge Bank pledgebank.com
Post Secret postsecret.com
Print & Pattern printpattern.blogspot.com
Prix Pictet prixpictet.com
Psychology Today psychologytoday.com

R

Red Magazine redonline.co.uk
Red Lemon Club redlemonclub.com
Republic republic.org.uk
Respect Women respectwomen.ca
Revolution.is revolution.is
Right to play righttoplay.com
Rock The Vote rockthevote.com
Roseissa roseissa.com
Royal Society for the Arts rsa.org
Row 6 row6.com
Ruby Fair rubyfair.com
Rules To Dress By elegancerebellion.com
Ryan Holiday ryanholiday.net

S

Sass Brown Blog ecofashiontalk.com/blog
Schmulb schmulb.com
Scoutie Girl scoutiegirl.com
See Africa Differently seeafricadifferently.com
September Rose september-rose.co.uk
Seth's Blog sethgodin.typepad.com
Showroom Workstation showroomworkstation.org.uk
SHOWstudio showstudio.com
Singularity Hub singularityhub.com
Sister Snog socialsnog.com
Six Magazine six-magazine.co.uk
Slavery Footprint slaveryfootprint.org
So & So so.andso.co
Social Design Site socialdesignsite.com
Society6 society6.com
Soko Kenya sokosite.com
Source Map sourcemap.com
SPARK+METTLE sparkandmettle.org.uk
Spiked spiked-online.com
Springwise springwise.com
Stitch project stitchproject.com
Story Corps storycorps.org
Strictly Writing strictlywriting.blogspot.com
Stumble Upon stumbleupon.com
Sublime Magazine sublimemagazine.com
Sunlight Foundation sunlightfoundation.com
Suno sunony.com
SustainWeb sustainweb.org

T

Techmeme techmeme.com
TED ted.com
Teen: dreaming hiyalouise.blogspot.com
Tellus Institute tellus.org
The 99% the99percent.com

The Akabusi Charitable Trust	akabusitrust.org
The Alligator	thealligatoronline.com
The Beat That My Heart Skipped	thebeatthatmyheartskipped.co.uk
The Big Give	thebiggive.org.uk
The British Guide To Showing Off	britishguidetoshowingoff.com
The Carl Sagan Portal	carlsagan.com
The Christian Socialist Movement	thecsm.org.uk
The Cultural Expose	theculturalexpose.co.uk
The Daily Mash	thedailymash.co.uk
The Economist	economist.com
The Eden Project	edenproject.com
The Edible Bus Stop	theediblebusstop.org
The Equity Trust	equalitytrust.org.uk
The Fawcett Society	fawcettsociety.org.uk
The Fox Is Black	thefoxisblack.com
The Funding Network	thefundingnetwork.org.uk
The Future We Want	futurewewant.org
The FWA	thefwa.com
The Green Backyard	thegreenbackyard.com
The Guardian	guardian.co.uk
The Hub	the-hub.net
The Huffington Post	huffingtonpost.com
The Imaginary Foundation	imaginaryfoundation.com
The Independent	independent.co.uk
The Internet is My Religion	internetismyreligion.com
The IPCC	ipcc.ch
The Long Now	longnow.org
The MIT Media Lab	media.mit.edu
The New Economics Foundation	neweconomics.org
The New York Times	nytimes.com
The Oatmeal	theoatmeal.com
The Onion	theonion.com
The Outdoor Swimming Society	outdoorswimmingsociety.com
The Paris Review	theparisreview.org
The Poetry Archive	poetryarchive.org
The Real Utopias Project	ssc.wisc.edu/RealUtopias
The School of Life	theschooloflife.com
The School for Designing a Society	designingasociety.org
The Slow Textiles group	slowtextiles.blogspot.com
The World Wildlife Fund	wwf.org.uk
The Writers Hub	writershub.co.uk
Theyec	theyec.org
The W Project	thewproject.co.uk
TheyWorkForYou	theyworkforyou.com
Thinking Flowers	thinkingflowers.org.uk
Things We Forget	thingsweforget.blogspot.com
ThirdSectorJobs	jobs.thirdsector.co.uk
This American Life - Time to Save The World (Radio)	thisamericanlife.org/radio-archives
Thought Questions	thoughtquestions.com
The Hunger Project	thp.org
Tim Ferriss' Blog	fourhourworkweek.com/blog
Timbuktu Chronicles	timbuktuchronicles.blogspot.com
Time Banks	timebanks.org
Tip The Planet	tiptheplanet.com/wiki
Topit.Me	topit.me
TRAID	traid.org.uk
Transition Town Totnes	transitiontowntotnes.org
TreeHugger	treehugger.com
Tristram Stuart WASTE	tristramstuart.co.uk
Tumblr	tumblr.com
Twitter	twitter.com
To Write Love On Her Arms	twloha.com
Typography Served	typographyserved.com

U, V

W

X, Y, Z

Future Soundtrack Playlist

All our contributors named a song to take with them to the future they choose. To listen via our spotify and you tube playlists, visit www.thefutureisbeautiful.co/future-soundtrack

A Change Is Gonna Come
—Otis Redding

A Minha Alma
—Marcelo Yuka

Accidental Babies
—Damian Rice

Across the Universe
—The Beatles

Alice
—Tom Waits

All I Ask
—Crowded House

All Things Must Pass
—George Harrison

All You Have Is Your Soul
—Tracy Chapman

All You Need Is Love
—The Beatles

Always On My Way Back Home
—Jay Jay Pistolet

Angie
—The Rolling Stones

Ants Marching
—Dave Matthews Band

Around the World
—Daft Punk

Baby
—Justin Bieber

Baby Can I Hold You
—Tracy Chapman

Back In Black
—AC/DC

Banana Pancakes
—Jack Johnson

Barbie Girl
—Aqua

Beat It
—Michael Jackson

Bedroom Eyes
—Natty

Believe
—Lenny Kravitz

Better Get To Livin
—Dolly Parton

Billy Jean
—Michael Jackson

Bitter Sweet Symphony
—The Verve

Black and Gold
—Sam Sparro

Blackbird
—The Beatles

Blind
—Hercules and Love Affair

Blood Buzz Ohio
—The National

Blowing In The Wind
—Bob Dylan

Body Is A Wonderland
—John Mayer

Bowl of Oranges
—Bright Eyes

Break and Enter
—Prodigy

Breakaway
—Kelly Clarkson

Bring Me Sunshine
—Morecambe & Wise

Bring Me To Life
—Katherine Jenkins

Broken
—Sam Clark

Brown Eyed Girl
—Van Morrison

Buffalo Gals
—Malcolm McLaren

Built to Last
—Sick Of It All

Bullet In The Head
—Rage Against The Machine

Caravan
—Van Morrison

Cattle and Creeping Things
—The Hold Steady

Cello Suite
—John Sebastian Bach

Ceremony
—New Order

Chain Gang
—Sam Cooke

Champagne Supernova
—Oasis

Change
—Tracy Chapman

Chhaiya Chhaiya (Dil Se)
—AR Rahman

Childhood Memories
— Ennio Morricone

Chop Suey
—System Of A Down

Cinnamon Girl
—Dunkelbunt

Commander
—Kelly Rowland feat. David Guetta

Common People
—Pulp

Could You Be Loved
—Bob Marley

Country Feedback
—REM

Credit Card Babies
—Men

Dam Mast qalander Mast Mast
—Nusrat Fateh Ali Khan

Dancing Cheek to Cheek
—Fred Astaire and Ginger Rogers

Dancing Nancies
—Dave Matthews Band

Das Model
—Kraftwerk

Daughters
—John Mayer

Days Like This
—Van Morrison

Destiny Calling
—James

Don't Burn Your Bridges
—Susan Cadogan

Don't Listen to a Word You've Heard
—Justin Nozuka

Don't Look Any Further
—Dennis Edwards

Don't Stop Believing
—Journey

Don't Stop Me Now
—Queen

Don't Worry Be Happy
—Guy Sebastian

Dream A Little Dream Of Me
—Ella Fitzgerald

Drive
—Incubus

E Prohibido Prohibir
—C.Veloso & Os Mutantes

Earth Song
— Michael Jackson

Emergency On Planet Earth
—Jamiroquai

Empire State of Mind
—Jay-Z & Alicia Keys

End Credits
—Chase and Status

Enjoy The Silence
—Depeche Mode

Enjoy Yourself
(It's Later Than You Think)
—The Specials

Everybody Loves The Sunshine
—Roy Ayers

Everloving
—Moby

Everything is Alright
—Four Tet

Evil
—Earth, Wind, and Fire

Fairy Tale Of New York
—The Pogues

Falling Leaves
—Pocketbooks

Fashion
—David Bowie

Fast Car
—Tracy Chapman

Feel
—Robbie Williams

Final Speech in The Great Dictator
—Charlie Chaplin

Fistful of Love
—Anthony And The Johnsons

Float On
—Modest Mouse

Gabriel's Oboe
—Ennio Morricone

Georgy Porgy
—Eric Benet and Faith Evans

Generator
—The Holloways

Get On Up
—James Brown

Girls Just Wanna Have Fun
— Cyndi Lauper

Give Peace a Chance
—John Lennon

God Will Make a Way
—Don Moen

Golden Brown
—Stranglers

Gonna Be An Engineer
—Peggy Seeger

Gonna Fly Now
—Bill Conti

Good Day Sunshine
—The Beatles

Good Old Fashioned Lover Boy
—Queen

Good Times Bad Times
—Led Zeppelin

Goodbye Horse
—Q Lazzarus

Grace
—Jeff Buckley

Great Salt Lake
—Band of Horses

Gypsy
—Shakira

Haegt Kemur Ljosio
—Olafur Arnalds

Hallelujah
—Jeff Buckley

Hallowed Be Thy Name
—Iron Maiden

Hand in Hand
—Koreana

*Har Ghari Badal Rahi
Hai Roop Zindagi -*
—Sonu Nigam

Hard Days Night
—The Beatles

Heard It Through The Grapevine
—Marvin Gaye

Hells Bells
—AC/DC

Here Comes The Sun
—The Beatles

Hey Soul Sister
—Train

Higher Ground
—Stevie Wonder

History Repeating
—Propellerheads & Shirley Bassey

Hitten
—Those Dancing Days

Home
—Michael Buble

Home is Where the Hatred Is
—Gil Scott-Heron

Hounds of Love
Kate Bush

Hurricane
—Bob Dylan

Hymn of Jesus
—Holst

I am here
—Jill Scott

I Believe in Miracles (You Sexy Thing)
—Hot Chocolate

I Don't Know What It Is
—Rufus Wainwright

I Feel Good
—James Brown

I Forgot To Be Your Lover
—William Bell

I Giorni
—Ludovico Einaudi

I Give Myself Away
—William McDowell

I Knew You Were Waiting For Me
—Aretha Franklin
and George Michael

I Want You (She's So Heavy)
—The Beatles

I Will Survive
—Gloria Gaynor

I'll Take Care Of You
—Gil Scott-Heron and Jamie XX

I'm Always Chasing Rainbows
—Judy Garland

I'm Yours
—Jason Mraz

I've Got You Under My Skin
—Ella Fitzgerald

If I Had A Hammer
—Sam Cooke

If I Had A Million Dollars
—The Barenaked Ladies

If You Want Me To Stay
—Sly and the Family Stone

Imagine
—John Lennon

Imma Be
—Black Eyed Peas

In The Deep
—Bird York

Infidelity
—Skunk Anansie

Into the Mystic
—Van Morisson

Into The Valley
—The Skids

Is Love Enough
—Michael Franti & The Spearheads

Is This It
—The Strokes

It Can Be Done
—Redskins

It Must Be Love
—Madness

It's No Good
—Depeche Mode

Jack Cheese and Bread snack
—Ott

Jealous Guy
—John Lennon

Jump Around
—House of Pain

Jump Rope
—Blue October

Jumper
—Third Eye Blind

Keep Myself Awake
—Black Lab

Keep Your Head Up
—Ben Howard

Killing In The Name
—Rage Against The Machine

Killing Me Softly
—The Fugees

King of the Mountain
—Kate Bush

La Valse D'Amelie
—Soundtrack to Amelie Poulain

Last
—Unthanks

Lazing On A Sunday Afternoon
—Queen

Le Vent Nous Portera
—Noir Desir

Let The Sunshine
—Labrinth

Like A Rolling Stone
—Bob Dylan

London Calling
—The Clash

Loose
—The Stooges

Lost In The Supermarket
—The Clash

Love Shack
—B52

Love Will Tear Us Apart
—Joy Division

Lovers In A Dangerous Time
—Barenaked Ladies

"Lysergic Bliss"
—Of Montreal

Make You Feel That Way
—Blackalicious

Man In The Mirror
—Michael Jackson

Mandarine Girl
—Booka Shade

Many of Horror
—Biffy Clyro

Masters of War
—Bob Dylan

Melek Yuzulum
—Mustafa Sandal

Memphis Soul Stew
—King Curtis

Mercy, Mercy Me
—Marvin Gaye

Misty Morning
—Bob Marley

MoneyGrabber
—Fits and the Tantrums

Movin On Up
—Primal Scream

Mr. Brightside
—The Killers

Musafir
—Dawood Sarkosh

My Love Has Gone
—Josh Rouse

My Way
— Frank Sinatra

Naked In The Rain
—Blue Pearl

Nature Boy
—Nat King Cole

Never Too Far
—Mariah Carey

Nights in White Satin
—The Moody Blues

Nightswimming
—REM

No Be Mistake
—9ice

No More Mr. Nice Guy
—Alice Cooper

No Woman No Cry
—Bob Marley

Northern Skies
—I Am Kloot

Not So Soft
—Ani DiFranco

Obladi Oblada
—The Beatles

On and On
—The Longpigs

One Day
—Matisyahu

One Day Like This
—Elbow

Only Skin
—Joanna Newsom

Peace Train
—Cat Stevens

People Help The People
—Cherry Ghost

Piano Concerto No.2
—Sergei Rachmaninoff

Picture In A Frame
—Tom Waits

Plastic Man
—The Kinks

Premier Gaou
—Magic System

Pretty Green Eyes
—Ultrabeat

Privacy
—Michael Jackson

Que Sera Sera
—Doris Day

Rainy Day
—Ayumi Hamasaki

Raspberry Beret
—Warren Zevon

Realize
—Part Time Heroes

Revolution
—The Beatles

Roadrunner
—Jonathan Richman
and The Modern Lovers

Run the World (Girls)
—Beyonce

Running Bear
—Johnny Preston

Salva Mea
—Faithless

Santeria
—Sublime

Satisfy My Soul
—Bob Marley

Sea, Sex and Sun
—Serge Gainsbourg

Send Me On My Way
—Rusted Root

Seven Wonders
—Fleetwood Mac

Sexual Healing
—Marvin Gaye

She's A Rainbow
—The Rolling Stones

Shipbuilding
—Robert Wyatt

Sign O' The Times
—Prince

Since I've Been Loving You
—Led Zeppelin

Singh Is Kinng
—Teri Ore

Sinnerman
—Nina Simone

Skinny Love
— Bon Iver

Slide Away
—Oasis

Slow
—Kylie Minogue

Smack My Bitch Up
—Prodigy

Smile
—Charlie Chaplin

Someone Like You
—Adele

Something Inside So Strong
—Labi Siffre

Somewhere Over the Rainbow
—Israel Kamakawiwo'ole

Somewhere Over The Rainbow
—Judy Garland

Song For The Dead
—Sea Wolf

Spinning Away
—Brian Eno & John Cale

Spiritual High (State of Independence)
—Moodswings

Star Star
—The Frames

Starlight
—Miho Fukuhara

Strange Fruit
—Billie Holiday

Superstition
—Stevie Wonder

Sweet Harmony
—The Beloved

Sweetheart Come
—Nick Cave

Sympathy For The Devil
—Laibach

Teardrop
—Massive Attack

Teenage Kicks
—The Undertones

Tequila
—Terrorvision

That's Amore
—Dean Martin

That's Life
—Frank Sinatra

The Departure
—Gattaca Soundtrack

The Dock of the Bay
—Otis Redding

The Drugs Don't Work
—The Verve

The End Is Where I Begin
—The Script

The Flower Duet
—Lakme

The Four Seasons
—Antonio Vivaldi

The Junkie Song
—The Be Good Tanyas

The Last Time I saw Richard
—Joni Mitchell

The Man Who Sold The World
—David Bowie

The Miller of Dee
—Folk Song

The Name Game
—Shirley Ellis

The Promise
—Tracy Chapman

*The Revolution
Will Not Be Televised*
—Gil Scott-Heron

*The Shanghai
Restoration Project*
—New Tea feat. Neocha EDGE

The Sunshine Underground
—Chemical Brothers

The Times Are Changing
—Bob Dylan

*The Village Green
Preservation Society*
—The Kinks

There Must Be An Angel
—The Eurythmics

This Boy
—The Beatles

This Magic Moment
—Lou Reed

Ticket To Ride
— The Beatles

Tiny Dancer
—Elton John

To Build A Home
—Cinematic Orchestra

To The East
—Electrelane

Top Secret
—Hangry and Angry

Trace A Line
—Au Revoir Simone

True Romance
—Citizens!

Try A Little Tenderness
—Otis Redding

Turning Japanese
—The Vapors

Unfinished Sympathy
—Massive Attack

Unorthodox
—Wretch 32

Unwritten
—Natasha Bedingfield

Visions of Paradise
—Mick Jagger

Waltz No.2
—Shostakoritch

Warsaw Concerto
—Richard Addinsell

Water No Get Enemy
—Fela Kuti

We
—Blasted Mechanism

We Are The World
—Michael Jackson

Wear Sunscreen
—Baz Luhmann

What A Beautiful Day
—Levellers

What A Wonderful World
—Louis Armstrong

What If Punk Never Happened?
—The King Blues

*What The World Needs
Now Is Love*
—Burt Bacharach & Traincha

What's Going On
—Marvin Gaye

When You Were Young
—The Killers

*Where The Streets
Have No Name*
—U2

Whoever Invented the Fishfinger
—Leon Rossellson

Wicked Game
—HIM

Wild Wood
—Paul Weller

Wishing On A Star
—Lionel Richie

Women of Hope
—Morley

Won't Get Fooled Again
—The Who

Wonderful World, Beautiful People
— Jimmy Cliff

Wonderland
—Sol Seppy

Wrecking Crew
—Overkill

Xerox
—Adam and The Ants

You Left The Water Running
—Otis Redding

You're The Voice
—John Farnham

You've Got The Love
—The Source feat. Candi Stanton

*Your Love Keeps Lifting Me (Higher
and Higher)*
—Jackie Wilson

You Can't Judge A Book
By The Cover
—Bo Diddley

Youth of Today
—Amy Macdonald

Acknowledgements

This book has been influenced and inspired by more people than we can mention. Firstly we would like to thank all of the people who have trusted us with their contributions and helped to make our little big idea a reality. Think Act Vote exists only thanks to the vibrant community of volunteers that have given to it just because they believe that it needs to exist in the world. It takes a village...

Thank you to Alexis Wieroniey for proof reading this book, and for encouraging the idea that first night in the pub alongside Poppy Whitfield. To Petronella Tyson, a core member of the team, who was there for every event. To Mark Bloom and Tony from Komodo, David Hawksworth and Becky Willan from Given London, and Jules Hau and Rosie Budhani from Foundation Agency, for all you did in those first three months.

Many thanks to all of the informal advisors to Think Act Vote for your words of wisdom, encouragement and your questions: Andy Gibson, Lauren Craig, Paul Hilder, Dan Snow, Ashish Ghadiali, Chris Erskine, James Parr, Jonathan Robinson, Sam Roddick, Lynne Franks and Annegret Affolderbach.

A big thank you to all who have helped behind the scenes at Think Act Vote: Christina Rebel, Christian Flores-Carignan, Iram Ramzan, Ikram Moundib, Tizane Navea-Rogers, Lina Jovaisaite, Laura Metcalf, Jo Keown, Shruti Duhan, Jasmeen Brar, Ravi Sodha, Jeremey Dillon, Kate Andrews and Ella Newton. And of course to the team behind this book who have inspired and humbled me and each other with their level of commitment and openness, and most importantly made the making of this book fun: Jo de Mornay Davies, Matthieu Becker, Kiran Patel, Gilly Rochester, Joana Casaca Lemos, Ella Britton, Dina Yunis, Amy Haworth Johns and Migle Vilkeliskyte.

In addition, I would like to thank Eddie Fitzpatrick, Romilly Dennys, Ellie Burrows, Lucie Barât, Chris Colston, Ashraf Saifullah, Chris Arnold, Tom Burke, Naïma Carthew, Vicky Fallon, Deniz Tekkul, Anne-Sophie Daba, Jesson Yip, Tuba Gursoy, Cyndi Rhoades, Katharine Hamnett, Tom Reeves, James Bridle, Lyla Patel, Steph Johnston, Oli Joseph, Sebastian Foot, Holly Berry, John Bird, Dominic Campbell, Hannah Carnell, Fatima Fazal, Deborah Doane, Ricardo Blaug, Neal Lawson, Emma Ponsonby, Jamie Burdett, Henry Hicks, Fiona Bennie, Susan Hepburn, Lola Young, Jim Woodall, Anna Fitzpatrick, Louise Kamara, Steve Brown, Karis McLarty, Laura Francis, Brian McKenney, Wayne Hemingway, Ed Gillespie and three dearly departed inspirations and friends, Gareth Huntley, Julia Thomson and Duncan Michael Wilson.

And finally thank you to my parents Himanshu and Hema Ghadiali for always encouraging me to ask the big questions, and for instilling in me the belief that each one of us makes a difference, and that what we do with our one precious life matters.

Amisha Ghadiali

The Book Team

Amisha Ghadiali - Editor & Creative Director
Amisha is a sustainable fashion activist, writer, yoga teacher and jewellery designer. She is fascinated with what makes us different and the same, and how we engage with nature and our surroundings. In addition to setting up the radical think tank Think Act Vote, Amisha is a trustee of the Foundation for Democracy and Sustainable Development and an elected member of the Electoral Reform Society council. Her work has been recognised by selection to the Cultural Leadership Programme and the Courvoisier Future 500, and by receipt of a Future 100 Award. She is currently working on a new concept www.replenish.world creating soulful retreats that give back to the local communties.
Future Soundtrack: Movin' on Up by Primal Scream
www.amisha.co.uk

Matthieu Becker – Designer
Matthieu is a French graphic designer working and living in London. He has an MA in Typography and Visual Art from ERG, Brussels. He runs a collective called LeMégot which creates zines, books and exhibitions. When he's not spending his time inside dusty bookshop basements or rummaging through bargain crates in record shops, Matthieu can be found working on the layout of books, editing videos and making music. He plays drums in his band 9m2.
Future Soundtrack: You Can't Judge A Book By The Cover by Bo Diddley
www.matthieubecker.com

Gilly Rochester – Editor
Gilly works variously as a teacher, an editor, copywriter and proofreader, and as an illustrator. Her main areas of interest are probably art and education and she spends quite a lot of time, whilst drawing or even proofreading, pondering such things as the nature of childhood and how it is changing with each generation; the impact of computers and the media; how and why successive governments seek to denigrate and ruin the wondrous teaching and learning that takes place in our state schools.
Future Soundtrack: Gabriel's Oboe by Ennio Morricone
www.gillyrochester.com

Kiran Patel (Illustrating Rain) – Illustrator
Kiran is an illustrator on a journey of creative alchemy, using the lines of form, shape and unfolding patterns to create imagery that envelops the eye. She has a background in sociology that remains an area of open curiosity. Interested in all things creative, she has a penchant for cooking, notebooks and spiritual development ... in no particular order. Kiran has a love for humour and wit as an asset for everyday life, and a belief that a belly laugh a day holds medicinal properties.
Future Soundtrack: Generator by The Holloways
www.illustratingrain.tumblr.com

Joana Casaca Lemos – Art Director
Joana is a communication designer (MA UAL) between Lisbon, London and the world. She is interested in the cultural, ethical and environmental intervention of the designer contribution to challenges of contemporary living, and has established an independent practice that implements responsible design principles to achieve creative outcomes. In 2011 Joanna worked in Thailand for The Doi Tung Sustainable Development Project. Keeping a close relationship with the academic sphere, she is currently a PhD research candidate. She is always eager and available to collaborate on projects towards new-age thinking and a healthy creative future.
Future Soundtrack: That's Life by Frank Sinatra
www.joanacasacalemos.com

Ella Britton – Art Director
Ella is a creative practitioner with a passion for social change, good design, and people. She has worked on a number of large social change projects and has developed new services and systems that continue to address some of today's biggest social challenges. She has developed community life-coaching services for families with complex needs, support systems for people with dementia, and new community engagement strategies for local authorities. She believes that creativity and hard work can be a force for tremendous social good.
Future Soundtrack: Dancing Cheek to Cheek by Fred Astaire and Ginger Rogers
www.thestriveforhappiness.wordpress.com

Amy Haworth Johns – Researcher
Amy is studying for her MA in Disasters, Adaptation and Development at King's College, London. Her studies have shaped her interest in social equality and inclusive participation, and she has worked on social projects in South Africa, Nicaragua, and across the UK. Currently living in her hometown London, she is re-immersing herself in the exciting vibes of London, hunting out vintage fairs, obscure nights and exciting restaurants. She is a keen explorer, getting itchy feet after too long a stint in the UK, and loves cooking up concoctions while loosely following recipes!
Future Soundtrack: Keep Your Head Up by Ben Howard
www.twitter.com/AMidilloHJ

Dina Yunis – Researcher
Dina is Lebanese, currently living in London and undertaking her MA degree in Environment, Politics, and Globalization at King's College London. She is a life enthusiast, a humanitarian and a photographer. She has a mind for graphics, animation, videos, sci-fi and a heart for old rock music, and travel. Dina works at the international peace education oriented NGO CISV as part of the Content section of the International Junior Branch Team, helping to organise information packs on current issues as well as regional and international conferences.
Future Soundtrack: Don't Listen To A Word You've Heard by Justin Nozuka
www.twitter.com/yunisd

Migle Vilkeliskyte – Researcher
Migle is a Lithuanian living in London and studying for an MA in Tourism, Environment, and Development at King's College London. She has completed a BA in Japanese Studies and spent 7 months studying Japanese language and culture in Tsukuba University, Japan. After graduating, she worked as a teacher in an international school. Migle is highly interested in many different cultures and loves travelling, photography and salsa dancing. She believes that small acts can make a big difference.
Future Soundtrack: La Valse D'Amelie by Yann Tiersen
www.twitter.com/MigureV

James Parr – Foreword
James is a product designer who has spent most of his career trying to figure out how to make multinationals more sustainable. He is co-founder of The Corporate Social Revolution Company, Imaginals.
Future Soundtrack: Gonna Fly Now by Bill Conti
www.imaginals.net

Samantha Roddick – Afterword
Sam is the founder of Coco de Mer, a British 'erotic emporium' dedicated to the celebration of sexual pleasure, empowerment, dignity and discovery. She is an activist for issues such as feminism, exploitation, and human rights.
Future Soundtrack: Everloving by Moby
www.twitter.com/samroddick

Contributors Index

Contributors Index

Afterword

The imagination is the constellation of our future. Each one of us is a ship, navigating the seas towards the destination of unborn generations.

To dream is the stepping stone to where we are going. We can't underestimate the power to imagine, as in truth, without dreaming nothing would be conceived.

An idea is nothing without action, but action is blind chaos without an idea.

At school I was taught that an ordinary individual with an average intelligence isn't powerful enough to shape global destiny. I was taught that only a chosen few have the capacity to the lead the world to our future. I was taught it takes a visionary and an extraordinary person to be powerful enough to make something remarkable happen.

All I was taught is a lie.

It is ordinary people, with a simple shift in attitude and a quiet resolved belief, who have changed the world; and who continue to make where we live a better place.

It is the common small act of kind generosity that is the catalyst to dramatic positive change.

We are all capable of changing our world. And we all equally play an important role in how our world exists.

Each one of us is brilliant enough - to search under the cobblestones of our restricted minds; to join together and turn the tide of where we are heading. We all have the capacity, we all have the intelligence, we all have the imagination to dream.

If we can allow each one of our cautious minds to wander down the corridors of possibility, then it is true that we can etch new heavens, and the stars, into the foundations of our own existence.

Anything is possible, even the impossible; we just have to dare to dream and take that small step into believing it is possible.

We must believe, think, act and vote to create a beautiful future.

Sam Roddick

Thank you for reading this book. We hope that you enjoyed experiencing it as much as we enjoyed making it. Please do share your answers to The Futures Interviews online and bring them into your conversations and your life.

We would love to know what you have thought about or discovered from our book and the ways it has impacted your daily life. Write to us. Connect.

This project has been a real labour of love. We chose to make the ebook free and the printed books as accessible as possible because you can't put a price on this work, and because we didn't want this beautiful future to be in any way exclusive. If you have got something from this book, please do help us to grow and bloom.

You can do this by making a donation which will allow us to put resources into getting the book in front of more peope, or you can simply share the book, in any way that you can. Send it out to everyone you know, write about it or get it featured, post it on social media, find us places where we can come and give a talk or run a workshop. Review it online. Give it as a gift. Unleash your imagination.

Help us to spread the word so we can build our global community of individuals - thinking, acting and voting together to create the beautiful future.

You are Beautiful. You are The Future.

www.thefutureisbeautiful.co/share

#TheFutureIsBeautiful

connect@thefutureisbeautiful.co
www.thefutureisbeautiful.co
www.facebook.com/thinkactvote
www.twitter.com/thinkactvote
www.pinterest.com/thinkactvote
www.instagram.com/thefutureisbeautiful

THE FUTURE IS BEAUTIFUL
A Collection From Think Act Vote

Printed in Great Britain
by Amazon